W9-BLD-981

World War II

LIFE OF AN AMERICAN SOLDIER IN EUROPE

by John F. Wukovits

Lucent Books, P.O. Box 289011, San Diego, CA 92198-9011

Titles in The American War Library series include:

World War II
Hitler and the Nazis
Kamikazes
Leaders and Generals
Life as a POW
Life of an American Soldier in Europe
Strategic Battles in Europe
Strategic Battles in the Pacific
The War at Home
Weapons of War

The Civil War
Leaders of the North and South
Life Among the Soldiers and Cavalry
Lincoln and the Abolition of Slavery
Strategic Battles
Weapons of War

To Tom Buell, Friend and Mentor

Library of Congress Cataloging-in-Publication Data

Wukovits, John F., 1944–
Life of an American soldier in Europe / John F. Wukovits.
p. cm.—(American war library: World War II)
Includes bibliographical references and index.
Summary: Examines the lives of American infantrymen in Europe during World War II, describing their fears, combat experiences, leisure activities, homecomings, and more.
ISBN 1-56006-666-0 (lib. bdg. : alk. paper)
1. World War, 1939–1945—Psychological aspects—Juvenile literature. 2. World War, 1939–1945—Campaigns—Western Front—Juvenile literature. 3. Soldiers—United States—Psychology—Juvenile literature. 4. United States Army—Military life—Juvenile literature. [1. World War, 1939–1945—Europe. 2. United States Army—Military life. 3. Soldiers—Psychology.] I. Title. II. Series.
D756.3.W85 2000
940.54'1273 21—dc21 99-042767
CIP

P.O. Box 289011, San Diego, California 92198-9011

Printed in the U.S.A.

☆ Contents ☆

★ Foreword ★

A Nation Forged by War

The United States, like many nations, was forged and defined by war. Despite Benjamin Franklin's opinion that "There never was a good war or a bad peace," the United States owes its very existence to the War of Independence, one to which Franklin wholeheartedly subscribed. The country forged by war in 1776 was tempered and made stronger by the Civil War in the 1860s.

The Texas Revolution, the Mexican-American War, and the Spanish-American War expanded the country's borders and gave it overseas possessions. These wars made the United States a world power, but this status came with a price, as the nation became a key but reluctant player in both World War I and World War II.

Each successive war further defined the country's role on the world stage. Following World War II, U.S. foreign policy redefined itself to focus on the role of defender, not only of the freedom of its own citizens, but also of the freedom of people everywhere. During the cold war that followed World War II until the collapse of the Soviet Union, defending the world meant fighting communism. This goal, manifested in the Korean and Vietnam conflicts, proved elusive, and soured the American public on its achievability. As the United States emerged as the world's sole superpower, American foreign policy has been guided less by national interest and more on protecting international human rights. But as involvement in Somalia and Kosovo prove, this goal has been equally elusive.

As a result, the country's view of itself changed. Bolstered by victories in World Wars I and II, Americans first relished the role of protector. But, as war followed war in a seemingly endless procession, Americans began to doubt their leaders, their motives, and themselves. The Vietnam War especially caused people to question the validity of sending its young people to die in places where they were not particularly wanted and for people who did not seem especially grateful.

While the most obvious changes brought about by America's wars have been geopolitical in nature, many other aspects of society have been touched. War often does not bring about change directly, but acts instead like the catalyst in a chemical reaction, accelerating changes already in progress.

Some of these changes have been societal. The role of women in the United States had been slowly changing, but World War II put thousands into the workforce and into uniform. They might have gone back to being housewives after the war, but equality, once experienced, would not be forgotten.

Likewise, wars have accelerated technological change. The necessity for faster airplanes and a more destructive bomb led to the development of jet planes and nuclear energy. Artificial fibers developed for parachutes in the 1940s were used in the clothing of the 1950s.

Lucent Books' American War Library covers key wars in the development of the nation. Each war is covered in several volumes, to allow for more detail, context, and to provide volumes on often neglected subjects, such as the kamikazes of World War II, or weapons used in the Civil War. As with all Lucent Books, notes, annotated bibliographies, and appendixes such as glossaries give students a launching point for further research. In addition, sidebars and archival photographs enhance the text. Together, each volume in The American War Library will aid students in understanding how America's wars have shaped and changed its politics, economics, and society.

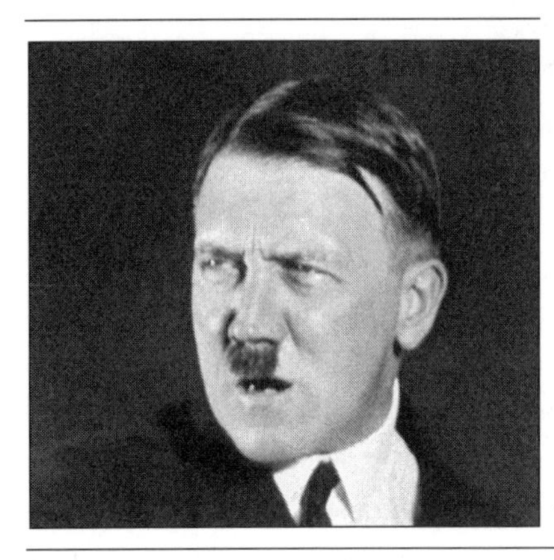

☆ Introduction ☆

"The Sharp End"

In the summer of 1998 vast numbers of Americans attended Steven Spielberg's latest release, *Saving Private Ryan.* The movie, about a platoon of combat soldiers sent on a mission to locate and remove from battle the sole surviving son of a midwestern family, showed in graphic detail what battle was like for the World War II soldier. The film tossed a relentless sequence of torn limbs, shattered faces, and scared young men at the moviegoers. Spectators left in stunned silence, alone with their thoughts about what they had just seen.

One group shuffled out silently because, as veterans of the war, old memories were reawakened and their consciousness flooded with images of friends lost and battles waged.

Others, the younger people and those who had never seen combat, walked out of theaters with both a sense of shock over what these men had endured and a sense of respect that they were able to endure it. War had not been handed to them in a harmless video game or a sanitized Hollywood production; a sliver of the real war, not the "good" war, appeared on screen.

In a scene from Saving Private Ryan, *a soldier tries to comfort a terrified girl as his platoon battles German troops in her village. The film graphically showed the horrors of combat.*

Gung Ho Soldiers

A similar sudden awareness had occurred almost fifty years earlier, not in the theaters but at the French beaches on D day, on the shores of Italy at Anzio, and in the frigid winter of 1944 near Germany. In November 1941 young men throughout the United States thought they knew what war was like. Having no personal experience of the battlefield, most men viewed war as noble and energizing.

The movies then, as they generally do today, presented war as an exciting adventure. Heroes rose to the forefront in epic encounters between good and evil, whether set in Elizabethan England, during the American Civil War, or in Europe in 1918. Farsighted generals carefully planned the battles and willing soldiers enthusiastically carried out the orders in organized fashion. When soldiers died, they died cleanly—a speedy thrust of the saber into a stomach or a single bullet to the chest, neither of which made a visible mark on the victim. Mortally wounded, the dying fighter clutched his wounds and dropped slowly to the ground. After muttering a few last words to a comrade who had gently cradled him in his arms, the soldier passed away without as much as a single bloodstain marring the terrain.

When World War II approached, the young men who left home and headed to training camp carried these notions of the battlefield with them. War, though dangerous, carried nobility and valor. An added bonus was that during World War II, American soldiers battled Adolf Hitler. No doubt existed that the German leader was the

During World War II, the young Americans headed for training camp thought of themselves as the good guys who would save the world from Adolf Hitler.

twentieth-century equivalent of the devil. The good guys from the United States intended to figuratively ride over the hill and, like a cavalry charge, swoop down to destroy the bad guys.

Training camp handed the new soldiers their first indication that war would be no parade. Intense drills, physical agonies, and mental torment toughened the men, but they still believed that battle would be glorious. Since days and nights of maneuvers and marches produced few casualties, the men still retained their wholesome image of war. Some even worried that the war would end before they reached foreign shores. Army private Morton Eustis explained that he was "so scared Germany may sue for peace before we have a chance to take a crack at her."[1]

Reality Protrudes on Image

After an ocean voyage to Europe, the men entered battle for the first time. Their entire outlook altered in a second. Instead of organized assaults by large masses of men, the fighting broke down to hundreds of smaller conflicts fought among a handful of soldiers, each of whom knew nothing about what occurred elsewhere. Fear gripped everyone and paralyzed many. Most shocking was that soldiers did not die cleanly. Blood splattered the ground, and death was often neither immediate nor painless.

Soldier Anton Myrer recalled the moment he realized what was obvious to combat veterans but what had never been related to noncombatants.

> We had been seduced by the ermine and the crimson sashes, the boots and mustachios and spurs aglitter on parqueted floors, by cuirasseurs sweeping down sunlit vales in plumed, cloak-waving charge towards sparkling little brass cannon where the old purple-and-gold standard flutters gaily. Errol Flynn, in brief: Errol Flynn. The dashing, resplendent hero we have been led to ape—the hero that never did exist. We have been bewitched, all of us, by the seductive abstractions that have nothing whatever to do with a man . . . holding up to you his shattered stump of a leg and sobbing piteously his anguish and bewilderment.[2]

Glory, nobility, and valor quickly fled from the battlefield and were replaced with fear, panic, and suffering. To survive, the men had to quickly discard their outdated notions of war and deal with the reality that so cruelly slapped them. Heroes did exist but instead of riding over the crest on white horses, they shivered in wet foxholes or stumbled across shell-torn fields.

The Man at the Edge

In 1945 wartime cartoonist Bill Mauldin wrote that the infantry soldier placed his life in danger more frequently than any other segment of the military yet received less recognition. Sadly, Mauldin was more accurate than he probably realized. The men who deserved the most acclaim, because

In his cartoons, Bill Mauldin portrayed the infantry soldier as an unsung hero who faced danger and hardship for little recognition.

they did the fighting and the bleeding and the dying, received little notice.

For today's generations, however, *Saving Private Ryan* proved to be the most compelling work to give voice to the experience of the soldier. Because of the film, people became more aware of the World War II infantryman and his contributions. Granddaughters and grandsons quizzed aging grandfathers about their experiences; schools opened classroom doors to veterans; consumers flocked to bookstores to pick up volumes by Stephen Ambrose and other talented World War II writers.

Although generals create orders, it is the infantrymen who carry them out. Strategists formulate grand plans, but no plan can be successful without the blood and lives of foot soldiers who, though scared, rush forward to grapple with the enemy. Their stories fill these pages, the men who battled, as one historian put it, "at the sharp end"[3] of the military machine.

☆ Chapter 1 ☆

"I Can Take Anything"

From 1941 to 1945, 11 million young American males received the same letter. Sent by their local draft boards, the letters opened with the word "Greeting," then went on to explain that the men had just been selected to join the service. From that moment on, their lives would never be the same, for this letter was their introduction to war. Many would recall years later that, while they would never wish to repeat the experience ignited by the notification, they were happy that they had gone through it. Others would try to forget those years. Another group—too large in number—would leave home healthy and happy but return in a wooden coffin or physically or mentally maimed.

These men formed the backbone of the U.S. Army that fought World War II. They left homes, schools, families, and futures to battle Hitler's legions on European battlefields, and when the dust settled in 1945, they returned victorious.

Off to Camp

The fate of millions was decided by sixty-five hundred draft boards across the nation. Staffed by five prominent local citizens in their forties and fifties, each board examined the list of males in its town or city and decided who would be drafted to serve in the army.

Of the 11 million men drafted in World War II, 7 million were sent to the army. At first the draft boards refrained from selecting fathers, but as the war continued they were forced to include that group. Deferments were granted to workers in defense plants and in other occupations that were considered crucial, but most men understood that, sooner or later, the letter would arrive.

Once a man received the official notification, he traveled to an army reception center for early processing. This was where he first learned that the army was about to control his life. Uniforms were issued to each arriving group, and a typically gruff

Before their train leaves for camp, draftees bid their wives and children goodbye. In the first years of the war, fathers were exempt from the draft.

sergeant would ask whether everyone's uniform fit. One man recalled that "the Sergeant said if something could be buttoned it was not too tight. If it stayed with you when you stepped forward it was not too loose."[4]

The men then departed for one of the 242 training centers set up around the nation. Most were located in southern states, where training could occur on a year-round basis. The largest facility, Fort Benning in Georgia, could train ninety-five thousand infantry soldiers at one time.

After listening to a lengthy list of offenses for which he could be punished, such as desertion and going absent without leave, the new soldier took the Army General Classification Test (AGCT). The soldier had forty minutes to answer 150 multiple-choice questions, which focused heavily on basic mathematics and synonym usage. Individuals fell into one of five categories, depending on the test score, ranging from Class I candidates (those who scored 130 and above) to Class V (those who scored 69 or less). The soldiers correctly assumed that the assignment they would receive with the army hinged on the outcome of this test, so they tried hard to get at least a score of 110, which qualified them for officer candidate school.

A fifteen-minute interview with a classification specialist followed. The soldier explained what he had done in civilian life, and the army specialist tried to match that experience with something similar in the service. While many men were placed in categories that suited their talents, others could find no logical reason for their assignments. Thus a garbage collector might wind up as a cook and a butcher as a medic, but on the whole the system worked fairly well.

One problem that complicated the assignment process was that in many cases the army required skills that few civilian occupations provided. General Lewis B. Hershey, the head of the Selective Service System, astutely pointed out that "I haven't seen a draft questionnaire yet in which the guy said he shot people for a living."[5]

After being sworn into the army (left), draftees trade their civilian clothes for uniforms (below).

Welcome to the Real Training, Guys

The army got right to the point. Private Ed Tipper learned in his early moments that expectations of an easy first day in camp were woefully far from reality. The one-thousand-foot Mount Currahee dominated the camp in which he trained. It sat like an ominous presence, undoubtedly waiting to provide a stern challenge later for the young men who would then be in improved physical condition.

"I looked up at nearby Mount Currahee and told someone, 'I'll bet that when we finish the training program here, the last thing they'll make us do will be to climb to the top of that mountain,'" mentioned Tipper. "A few minutes later, someone blew a whistle. We fell in, were ordered to change to boots and athletic trunks, did so, fell in again—and then ran most of the three miles to the top and back down again."[6] A handful of men dropped out of the run that day, but most held on. By week's end, the men were double-timing their way up Mount Currahee.

When the men were not running or doing calisthenics, they learned to march in unison. Constant drilling, which nearly every soldier detested, stretched interminably throughout the hot, humid Georgia days. Night marches followed, during which the men could not stop for water, cigarettes, or rest. An initial eleven-mile march increased by a mile or two each night. The commanding officer even checked each man's water canteen to make sure he did not drink any water during the march.

Obstacle courses winding through fields attempted to re-create some of the conditions the soldiers would face in combat. Eventually live ammunition was used. As soldiers hugged the ground, machine-gun bullets whizzed overhead and shells screamed to explosive ends. In two years of training, from 1942–1944, the army used 240,000 tons of ammunition and explosives.

The soldiers received their rifles during training. Officers warned the men to treat the item as their closest friend and admonished that if they took care of their rifles, their rifles would be there when they needed them most. The soldiers also learned how to disassemble and reassemble the weapons while blindfolded.

Dodging bullets, two soldiers crawl along an obstacle course. Live ammunition was used on courses like this to simulate battlefield conditions.

A Strange World

Training camp introduced young men to an alien world—that of the military. Having been accustomed to civilian ways all his life, the inductee had to quickly shift gears to cope with all the new and strange ways of doing things. In his book *If You Survive,* George Wilson, who served as a lieutenant in Europe, describes his initial feelings in training camp.

> For the next seven weeks we struggled through a basic infantry course, with the usual KP [Kitchen Police] and guard duties, with lectures on fundamentals such as military courtesy, some weapons training and actual firing on the rifle range, bayonet drill, and hand-to-hand combat. Everything was very new and strange to me. I had never been away from home for more than a week and was totally ignorant of the Army. At first I didn't know a corporal from a sergeant, and officers seemed like gods to me because everybody, including the sergeants, jumped to rigid attention when they appeared.

Inductees attend an outdoor lecture at training camp. They would have to master skills and situations that were not found in the civilian world.

As the men performed the various physical activities, they chanted in unison, shouted, and swore. The language drew together men from all sections of the nation and helped promote the solidarity so essential to combat. They may not have known each other a few days ago, but they were already being united by marching and singing, or by the hatred of army drills.

The men quickly learned to obey orders without question, for certain punishment followed if they did not. Although they lived in a democratic nation, they now existed in a dictatorial military arm, and training camp was where this fact was repeatedly emphasized. Practically every soldier had to endure twenty extra push-ups for a minor infraction, and most lost precious weekend passes or had to march in the field for several hours with full field pack.

When one man tossed a cigarette butt to the ground, his sergeant ordered him to dig a six-foot-deep hole to bury it in. Another man forgot to properly button his shirt and had to scrub the barracks for one week—with a toothbrush. This was all designed to promote unity and to instill the fact that a soldier must instantly obey an order. In training camp, a mistake cost a man extra physical exertion; in combat, it may cost his life.

When not in the field, the soldiers sat in classrooms to learn military courtesy, discipline, sanitation, and an array of other subjects deemed necessary by the army. They then advanced to the second phase of their training, in which they mastered the weapons used in their specialty, whether rifles, bazookas, machine guns, or tanks.

A typical day in training camp left little free time for the soldier. He awoke at 5:55 A.M. and had twenty-five minutes to wash, dress, make his bed, and fall in for roll. He then hurried to the mess hall for a twenty-minute breakfast, rushed back to his barracks to clean the area and prepare for the new day, then scampered to the field by 8:00. Almost ten hours of training followed, after which the exhausted soldier returned for a 6:00 P.M. supper. Lights out did not occur until 9:45, but each soldier had to clean his rifle and the area around his barracks. He might possibly squeeze out a letter to a girlfriend back home or to his family, but frequent night marches, kitchen duty, and guard duty made his free time uncertain.

Soldiers eventually cast aside civilian ways. A large number had brought a pair of pajamas to training camp, but these were soon discarded for sleeping army style, in their underwear. The men learned to do without the luxuries of home, although in some cases they considered army existence superior to what they had known. One soldier from a Texas farm wrote home that he loved the army because he could now sleep in until almost 6:00 A.M.

What most soldiers recalled about training, however, was the utter misery: Endless drills, constant physical exertion, and harassment from sergeants and lieutenants filled the day and haunted the nights. One soldier wrote to his family,

> I cannot picture everything clearly to you for I cannot send you a box of Texas dust to pour liberally over your whole body. I cannot send you a long, hot road and a fine set of blisters or a heavy pair of G.I. shoes to be broken

In the second phase of training, soldiers learned how to use their weapons. Here an infantryman practices using a bayonet.

> in. I cannot send you an over coat which you will not be allowed to wear at reveille [wake-up and roll call] when it is freezing, but which you will be required to wear during the sweltering afternoon.[7]

The worst came at the end. A soldier who endured the ordeal at Camp Gruber, Oklahoma, wrote,

> The culmination of physical training was the requirement that the soldier with rifle and thirty pound pack, negotiate a 1500 foot obstacle course in three and a half minutes. Specific requirements were that he take off with a yell [yelling or singing frequently accompanied physical activity], mount an eight foot wall, slide down a ten foot pole, leap a flaming trench, weave through a series of pickets, crawl through a water main, climb a ten foot rope, clamber over a five foot fence, swing by a rope across a seven foot ditch, mount a twelve foot ladder and descend to the other side, charge over a four foot breastwork, walk a twenty foot catwalk some twelve inches wide and seven feet over the ground, swing hand over hand along a five foot horizontal ladder, slither under a fence, climb another, and cross the finish line at a sprint.[8]

At the end of training at Camp Gruber, Oklahoma, soldiers had to traverse an obstacle course that included fences, poles, ropes, and flaming trenches (pictured).

Citizen Soldiers

The common element most combat units shared in World War II was, ironically, their diversity. National Guard outfits collected men from one area, but in a true display of equanimity, draftee divisions pulled in men from all corners of the nation. The "melting pot" image that marked the United States could be clearly seen in army draftee divisions.

In their riveting account of life in a rifle company, *The Men of Company K,* Harold P. Leinbaugh and John D. Campbell described the level of education the members of their company had obtained.

> Education varied. Like Brewer, Paul Coste was a Harvard man. Bruce Baptie came from Yale. Sergeants Erickson and Hadley were college graduates, and Magee had a law degree. Bill Chalmers, a former New York advertising executive, had originated the *Take It or Leave It* radio quiz program. At the other end of the scale were several men who could neither read nor write; friends wrote their letters home.[9]

Thus the typical combat soldier did not come from any particular section of the nation or from any social group. North and South, educated and illiterate, poor and middle class all served as what historian Stephen Ambrose called "citizen soldiers"—civilians who halted their normal peacetime occupations to eliminate the threat posed by Germany and Japan.

When it came to racial origin, however, the army abandoned the melting pot and perpetuated the segregation that existed in society at large. Though African Americans served in the war, few entered combat. Most filled support roles such as truck drivers or clerks. But on the whole, army draftee divisions claimed no one social class as their target. Instead, all served together.

A Family of Men

Gradually, the men began to consider their unit as family. Mom and dad, brother and sister, friends and sweethearts existed elsewhere; the soldiers sleeping in their barracks now formed their world. As Leinbaugh and Campbell explained,

> Nearly all the men were within a year of their twentieth birthday. The strong bonds of loyalty and friendship developed during those long, grueling months of backbreaking training . . . became even more important as the Railsplitters [their unit] traveled toward the front. Wives, parents, and children were . . . away. K Company was the only family we had. As apprehensions and anticipation grew, so grew the realization that whatever lay before us, we were in it together.[10]

The men shared experiences that outsiders could know little of and understand even less. Thus they drew close together and felt an unbreakable bond that connected one soldier with another. As Stephen Ambrose explained,

> Their trust in, and knowledge of, each other is total. They got to know each other's life stories, what they did before they came into the Army, where and

why they volunteered, what they liked to eat and drink, what their capabilities were. On a night march they would hear a cough and know who it was; on a night maneuver they would see someone sneaking through the woods and know who it was from his silhouette.[11]

All was designed to prepare men to face one of humanity's harshest requirements: to charge into battle to kill another human being. Those who could not adjust to training camp were removed, such as the man who froze on the obstacle course and the young boy who softly cried out for his mother at night. Drug addicts and blatant criminals drifted away. The rest, the ones who tolerated physical conditioning and hollering and loneliness, felt ready for battle. They believed they possessed superior skills to the enemy and that they would still act honorably when they faced death and injury.

For the Common Good

In training camp, the army tried to instill in soldiers pride in their unit and a willingness to do what was right for their buddies. Selfishness had no role. In his collection of articles about the war titled *This Was Your War*, Frank Brookhouser included a poem scribbled near the public telephone at one training camp.

> When calling Anne or Louise
> Don't dally by "shooting the breeze"
> Make your talk short and sweet
> Then beat a retreat
> So your buddies can call if they please.

Training ended with the men confident and prepared. Each understood the intricacies of his assigned task within the unit, whether it was in communications, as a machine gunner, or as a medic. They had absorbed enough training that, in an emergency, they believed they could take over the chores of any other man in the unit. "We all thought after this," said Private Burton Christenson, "I can take anything they can throw at me."[12]

Heading Overseas

At the completion of training camp, each man usually enjoyed a ten-day leave. Soldiers who had been untested boys only months before now returned in prime physical condition, exuding confidence and discipline. They then traveled to a staging area where the men assembled for the journey across the Atlantic.

The conditions aboard the troop transport left some men missing training camp. Without an adequate supply of fresh water, the men were forced to use seawater for showers. This produced typical gripes and groans, but it was a phenomenon they would shortly look back on with fondness. The sleeping accommodations in the compartments belowdecks were hot, stuffy, and crowded. Canvas and metal-frame bunks were suspended by chains and piled atop one another with barely two feet of space between. Soldiers could go up on deck during the daytime, but even there the crowded conditions became a nuisance.

Loaded with soldiers, a troop transport leaves for Europe. The crowded conditions aboard ship were in some cases worse than those found in training camp.

Most irritating, however, was the fact that officers received superior quarters. While the men sweated belowdecks, officers enjoyed larger rooms, more ventilation, and more comfortable bunks. The soldiers outnumbered officers seventeen to one, but the officers occupied half the space allocated aboard ship.

The daytime was filled with calisthenics, lectures, and leisure. An army information officer attempted to give background on the countries to which the men were traveling and explain what customs were acceptable there. Men heading toward North Africa, for instance, were warned not to kill snakes or birds because some Arabs believed they contained the souls of departed chieftains.

Shortly before boarding the troop transport, each soldier had received a letter from President Franklin D. Roosevelt wishing him good luck and thanking him for the work he was about to do. He appreciated the communication, even though it was a form letter, but wondered if the home front truly understood his feelings. As Stephen Ambrose wrote,

> They knew they were going into great danger. They knew they would be doing more than their part. They resented having to sacrifice years of their youth to a war they never made. They wanted to throw baseballs, not grenades, shoot a .22 rifle, not an M-1. But having been caught up in the war, they decided to be as positive as possible in their Army careers.[13]

★ Chapter 2 ★

"Our New-Boy Illusions . . . Dissolved"

The men who crossed the Atlantic Ocean and arrived in Europe had completed their training. They were about to enter battle as part of an invasion force and find out what it was like to attack another human being who was trying to kill them. Whether the men landed in North Africa in 1942, Italy in 1943, or France in 1944, the ordeal was basically the same. The soldiers stepped into battle as naive innocents. Those who survived emerged as different people.

D Day

One of the best examples of an invasion of soldiers occurred on the beaches of Normandy along France's northwest coast. On June 6, 1944, American, British, and Canadian troops landed against heavily fortified German positions to begin the mammoth drive across western and central Europe to the German homeland.

Military planners had scoured the European coastline for hundreds of miles for the best site to mount an invasion. Since the spring of 1940, Adolf Hitler's vaunted German Army had controlled much of Europe from France to the Soviet Union. If the Allied forces (the United States, Great Britain,

The first wave of soldiers goes ashore at Normandy. Their task was to destroy enemy machine guns and artillery positions.

and their allies) were to eventually defeat the Germans, they would have to begin with an attack from the sea against heavily fortified positions, one of the hardest military operations imaginable. They settled on Normandy for their opening drive.

A military invasion from the sea is meticulously planned. Soldiers come ashore in predesigned waves, or groups of men and matériel. The first wave, for instance, contains men whose task is to destroy enemy machine guns and artillery positions. Succeeding waves bring ashore engineers, additional infantry, staff headquarters, and other necessary items. If the attack on Normandy was to proceed as scheduled, the first waves had to hit the beaches, rush across, and attack the Germans defending the beaches from behind. The first wave could not afford to tarry on the beach because it would retard the landing of successive waves.

Allied soldiers hit Normandy at five different locations. One location, called Omaha Beach, typified the risks and horrors of mounting a seaward invasion against entrenched opposition. The area around Omaha Beach formed a perfect killing ground for the Germans. One-hundred-foot bluffs surrounded a narrow beach on three sides. At each end of the beach, the Germans housed large guns, called 88s, which could fire across the beach's entire length. Along the slopes of the bluffs, machine-gun positions and soldiers filling the trenches waited to hurl an incredible array of bullets, mortar shells, and grenades at the oncoming Allied troops. Each inch of beach had been presighted by German gunners to ensure that no matter where an Allied soldier stepped ashore, he would come under fire from more than one weapon. The only way a soldier could get off the beach was to scurry to one of several small depressions about one-hundred yards wide, which the Germans had ringed with barbed wire and planted with hundreds of land mines.

Before even reaching the beach, though, American troops on approaching landing craft had to navigate through a series of six-pronged iron obstacles resting barely beneath the water's surface. Each arm of the obstacles bore a mine containing enough explosive force to wreck the landing craft.

Bloody Omaha Beach

American soldiers recognized the seriousness of their task long before the first wave crashed ashore. Nerves knotted stomachs and dried lips. Men became seasick because the choppy waters of the English Channel buffeted the landing craft. All one could do was bear the agony in silence and be comforted with the knowledge that he did not suffer alone. Hopefully, once on land they could push aside light opposition and get some rest.

That was wishful thinking, for the soldiers in those landing craft sped toward a beach bristling with German weaponry. When a German officer first spotted the Americans chugging directly toward his beach, he exclaimed, "They must be

At Omaha Beach, the Germans used guns like this 88 to pound the invading Americans. The guns helped make the beach a perfect killing ground.

crazy. Are they going to swim ashore? Right under our muzzles?"[14]

One young soldier, Private H. W. Shroeder, would have agreed with the Germans as his boat neared the shore. As he huddled below the metal sides for protection, he heard "noises on the side of the landing craft like someone throwing gravel against it."[15] When his and other boats hit the shore, the front ramps lowered, exposing every man inside to withering machine-gun fire. Men slumped to the deck, splashed into the water, and, mortally wounded, fell back on the soldiers behind them. In more than one craft men were shot through the head as soon as the ramps lowered. One boat completely disappeared in an eruption that vaporized all on board.

To avoid the horrendous fire, soldiers jumped over the sides into the water. Because the water's depth was eight feet or deeper in some places, men drowned before they could remove their heavy backpack and other equipment. Others crouched low in shallower water and inched forward. The *rrrip* of machine-gun bullets, the whine of 88 shells, the crash of big guns from both the Germans and American naval ships, and the thumping of mortars mixed with the shouts of officers and the cries of the wounded and dying.

Sergeant Thomas Valance was typical of the men at Omaha Beach. After being hit by a bullet in his left thigh, he suffered two more superficial wounds. Bullets smacked into his backpack twice without injuring him, and another shot away the chin strap to his helmet. He finally struggled up the beach and collapsed, the only survivor of his unit of thirty men. "The bodies of my buddies were washing ashore and I was the only one live body in amongst so many of my friends, all of whom were dead, in many cases very severely blown to pieces."[16]

At Omaha, soldiers dodge enemy bullets as they crawl between obstacles. So many Americans died here that the beach later resembled a slaughterhouse.

Bodies without heads or limbs littered the beach. Soldiers cried for help or begged for their mothers. Men carrying flamethrowers erupted in a fiery ball after being hit by a bullet; others were killed as they huddled next to an iron obstacle. Some soldiers wet their pants in fright, while others stared at the ground in terror.

The fearsome carnage had to be endured, though, if the soldiers were to take Omaha Beach. In isolated spots, officers and men rose to the challenge. Colonel George Taylor yelled at the men huddled on the beach, "There are only two kinds of people on this beach: the dead and those about to die. So let's get the hell out of here!"[17]

Gradually, men left their spots and rushed forward. Private Raymond Howell figured that if he were going to die, he may as well die fighting. After a few hours, enough men had reached the bluffs' tops to start eliminating German strongholds and secure Omaha Beach.

One soldier gazed back after the fighting and stood speechless. The bodies and debris on the beach reminded him of the Chicago stockyard cattle pens and the slaughterhouses that killed the animals for market.

Fear and Noise

As Normandy showed, in any battle's earliest moments, each soldier came to grips with fear. He wondered if he could be afraid and still be effective or if he would collapse and be useless to himself and his buddies. The soldier fresh from training could listen to tales from veteran soldiers, but until he experienced combat and realized that someone else was actually trying to kill him, the youth had no idea what combat was actually like.

Combat's early moments proved so alien to expectations that many soldiers experienced confusion and bewilderment.

One soldier later wrote of his first moments in France, "Panic came over me and for a wild moment I thought of marching into the new Company Commander's tent and saying, 'Look. There's been some big mistake. I'm here, but I haven't had the same training as the others and I have no idea what to do in combat. What do you intend to do about it?'"[18]

Then there was the noise. Combat engineer Henry Giles shivered in his foxhole on the Anzio beachhead in Italy while a German artillery bombardment crashed all around him. He said that one shell "got louder and louder until it was right on top of us and a thousand boxcars with locomotives attached couldn't have been noisier. . . . Then we heard a thud and I came as close to dying from fear as I ever will."[19]

Machine-gun bullets ricocheted off rocks, trees, and men's helmets. Rifle bullets zipped through the air, hit the ground with a frightening smack, and tore into uniform and flesh. Hand grenades exploded, bazooka and mortar shells swooshed toward targets, and aircraft bombs plunged down with a demonic screech.

The Sound of Soldiers Crying

Most soldiers realized that to attempt to describe to civilians what battle was like was nearly impossible. A few tried to convey what they experienced, however. In his book *The Deadly Brotherhood,* John McManus included the following powerful letter written from a soldier named Walter Slatoff to his son.

> My Son: War is a more terrible thing than all the words of man can say; more terrible than a man's mind can comprehend. It is the corpse of a friend, one minute ago a living human being with thoughts, hopes and a future just exactly like yourself—now nothing. It is the groans and the pains of the wounded, and the expressions on their faces. It is the sound of new soldiers crying before battle; the louder sound of their silence afterwards. It is the filth and itching and hunger; the endless body discomfort; feeling like an animal; the fatigue so deep that to die would be good. It is the evil, snickering knowledge that sooner or later the law of averages will catch up with each soldier, and the horrible hope that it will take the form of a wound, not maiming or death. Remember what we are talking about. Not words, not soldiers, but human beings just exactly like yourself.

Soldiers found it difficult to describe to civilians the fears and emotions they experienced in battle.

One of the most feared German weapons was the 88mm (millimeter) artillery, which hurled shells at the Americans faster than the speed of sound. Since the shell arrived before the sound it produced, the soldier's first indication that an 88 had zeroed in on his position was the bone-rattling explosion from the shells hitting. No combat soldier could relax with an 88 in the neighborhood.

Many soldiers believed that they would crack under the intense artillery barrages orchestrated by the enemy and felt that each shell sped straight toward them. Private Arnold Parish and his buddy were starting to dig their foxhole during the Battle of the Bulge in late 1944 when a German barrage interrupted. "It was raining shells and they were exploding all around our hole. The air was full of shrapnel and spent pieces were hitting us as we laid on our backs with our helmets over our faces. The noise was unbearable and the ground was shaking and we were shaking from fright and cold. We didn't dare raise our heads."[20]

Few soldiers anticipated the amount of screaming they encountered on the battlefield. Men screamed because they were wounded and cried out for medical assistance; others screamed from terror. These sounds blended in with other battlefield sounds. Some soldiers screamed when they charged and screamed when they took refuge under a barrage. Some screamed for their mothers; others screamed to get away.

Shattered Illusions

Before their first battle, soldiers carried the illusion that, once in combat, they would see their enemy, fight him, defeat him, and move on. Although this did sometimes occur, the opposite more frequently happened. Modern technology enabled both sides to fire at each other without actually being in sight.

Instead of relying on battlefield skills absorbed in training, Americans felt helpless against a hidden, impersonal enemy. Whom do you shoot against in an artillery barrage? In which direction do you point your weapon if no target offers itself? Audie Murphy, the most decorated American soldier of World War II, mentioned of the fighting in southern France that "Maybe my notions about war were all cockeyed. How do you pit skill against skill if you cannot even see the enemy?"[21]

German mines and booby traps added to the helplessness felt by soldiers. Most artillery shells (except for the feared 88) made noise, but mines gave no telltale sign of their presence. Mines were thin metallic or plastic plates that were buried barely beneath the soil and covered with twigs, leaves, and dirt. An advancing soldier never knew where one might be. At any moment an explosion might rip into the soldier from underneath.

Germans attached booby traps to almost everything. Americans had to be cautious of dead bodies or unconscious soldiers lying on battlefields because a wire might detonate an explosion when someone moved

Modern technology made it possible for units such as this American artillery crew to fire upon enemy positions that they could not see.

the body. Possible souvenirs, such as German weapons or pictures of Adolf Hitler, were favorite places for enemy booby traps. Americans despised these weapons because they had no one whom they could retaliate against; instead of a visible soldier, the mine or booby trap did all the damage.

The brutal initiation experienced by American soldiers taught them that they had much to learn, and even more to fear, than they had imagined. "Our new-boy illusions of the past two days dissolved in a moment,"[22] wrote Leinbaugh and Campbell of their opening encounter near the German border.

Facing Death

Mud and misery, artillery and mines, and the constant threat of death produced a shock the first time the American soldier entered battle. World War II was fought mainly by young men between the ages of eighteen and twenty-two, a time when dying should have been far from their minds. But suddenly they were forced to confront death with sickening clarity.

At first most men assumed they would not be killed; wounded possibly, but not killed. In a classic tale that often appears in World War II literature, a commander addresses his troops before entering battle. He explains that the operation is so risky that by the next morning every man, except one, will be dead. Each man supposedly looks at the rest of the unit and thinks, "Those poor fellows."

Whether true or fictional, the tale emphasizes that most soldiers headed into battle with an optimistic view. They assumed they would survive, return home, and resume their lives. Even training camp reinforced such notions. One soldier, Grady Gallant, mentioned, "The thought of dying had not occurred to [the soldiers]. They had not been taught to die. They had been taught to kill. Dying had not occurred to them. They did not look upon war as dying. War was killing."[23]

The error of this assumption came to a speedy crash once the soldier experienced his first combat and realized that a bullet

A Final Letter Home

Facing death every day on the line made soldiers more aware that each moment could be their last. Some shrugged off the thought with a fatalistic view that they could do nothing anyway, so why worry? Others wrote letters to their families to be opened only in the event of their deaths. John McManus included one such letter in his book, *The Deadly Brotherhood.*

> When you begin to face the very basic things in life, you don't mind speaking your heart. I want to thank you for all those thousands and thousands of little things which really make up life—when you, Dad, used to wait for us in the morning to take us to school . . . and wait again after school; and when you, Mom, would sit up at night until all of us were in bed. Though I would never be capable of full payment, I was hoping to do something for you some day. I had hoped to do it at home, but God has other plans. I want you to know that I'll be praying and waiting for you. Please don't have any regrets. God bless you and goodbye for now."

Shortly after writing this letter, the soldier was killed in action in Italy.

A soldier's helmet and rifle mark his grave somewhere in Europe.

could just as easily tear into an American as it could a German. One paratrooper who saw comrades die in France remarked,

> People didn't crumple and fall like they did in Hollywood movies. They were tossed in the air. They were whipped around. They were hit to the ground hard and their blood spattered everywhere. And a lot of people were standing close to people and found themselves covered in the blood and flesh of their friends, and that's a pretty tough thing for anybody to handle.[24]

Upon his initial sight of death, the soldier finally realized that another man, bearing similar weapons of destruction, wanted to kill him. Before, he had been the killer, but now he understood that his own existence was very much in doubt. As Grady Gallant stated,

> My own death had never been considered by me. But now, that very real possibility flooded my mind with crystal clarity. . . . It came to me that a [German] would no more hesitate to kill me than I would hesitate to slay him. He *would.* I could expect no mercy. There would be no negotiation. It would either be I would kill him, or he would kill me.[25]

Reaction

Men who had entered the European conflict with confidence now wondered if they would outlast the war. Confused and concerned that battle was not at all like training had taught them to believe, the soldiers had to readjust their frames of mind.

The first casualty was horseplay and boasting. The 16th Infantry Regiment battled a hardened German foe through North Africa and Sicily before being sent to England to prepare for the June 6, 1944, invasion of the European mainland. For purposes of security, the men were ordered not to disclose that they had been in combat, but citizens of a neighboring village, who had already experienced their own sons returning from battle, immediately spotted the difference between the 16th and raw troops. The raw troops bragged about how good they were and acted as if they owned the town. The 16th quietly moved about and kept out of sight.

Another method of dealing with combat was for soldiers to force its sounds and sights out of their minds. They pretended that what they saw had not happened or that they were a sheltered spectator to a ghoulish show. Soldiers tried to shove all emotion out of their consciousness. As if zombies shuffling about with vacant stares, they tried to numb themselves to events around them. One soldier along the German border contended that "all men in combat must come to [insensitivity]. To feel sorrow, to grieve for the dead, to weep in despair, was not what we were asked to do. To kill, to maim, to destroy, to die, these were our tasks, and we were to do them without too much fuss."[26]

At Normandy, soldiers have marked a comrade's body with crossed rifles. Training did little to prepare men for the realities of combat.

Repeated exposure to war's grimness produced another phenomenon. The soldiers aged rapidly. Faces that at first looked like they belonged in soda fountains and school dances took on harsh, weathered appearances. Lines etched through grimy faces. One veteran said, "Going [into battle], they are young and in the best of health. Returning, they are old and beaten shells that once were men."[27]

Many assumed what has been labeled the thousand-yard stare. Rather than gazing at a person, the soldiers appeared to be staring off at something a long distance away.

A Matter of Luck

Instead of thinking about the possibility of their own deaths, soldiers sidestepped it by concluding that there was little they could do to avoid it anyway. In large measure, they thought, luck determined their fate. After all, how many times did a shell explode and kill one man while leaving the man next to him untouched? "It's luck, pure and simple, this game," Morton Eustis wrote to his mother of his combat in France. "There's no other way you can look at it." He added that he hoped the war ended soon, "as your luck can hold out just so long in this type of game, and sooner or later someone's aim is going to be good, especially when you are sitting out most of the time in the point [lead] vehicle."[28] Viewing death this way took the burden off a soldier's shoulders and placed it on something he could not control—luck.

One popular belief was that an enemy bullet either had your name on it or did not. What you did in combat had little to

"I Love the Infantry"

Celebrated war correspondent Ernie Pyle, whose accurate descriptions of life for the combat soldier earned him the gratitude of every infantryman, brought the fighting war to the men and women back home. In the following, reprinted in Frank Brookhouser's *This Was Your War,* Pyle relates life for the soldier.

> I love the infantry because they are the underdogs. They are the mud-rain-frost-and-wind boys. They have no comforts, and they even learn to live without the necessities. And in the end they are the guys that wars can't be won without. . . .
>
> The men are walking. They are fifty feet apart, for dispersal. Their walk is slow, for they are dead weary, as you can tell even when looking at them from behind. Every line and sag of their bodies speaks their inhuman exhaustion.
>
> On their shoulders and backs they carry heavy steel tripods, machine-gun barrels, leaden boxes of ammunition. Their feet seem to sink into the ground from the overload they are bearing.
>
> They don't slouch. It is the terrible deliberation of each step that spells out their appalling tiredness. Their faces are black and unshaved. They are young men, but the grime and whiskers and exhaustion make them look middle-aged.
>
> In their eyes as they pass is not hatred, not excitement, not despair, not the tonic of their victory. There is just the simple expression of being there as if they had been doing that forever, and nothing else.

Correspondent Ernie Pyle described the infantryman's experience to the men and women at home.

do with your survival—it was already determined if your time was up. Another was to think in terms of a lottery, that if your number was up, you would die. It did not matter whether the action he faced was relatively small or extremely risky. A soldier need not worry because the outcome had already been decided.

Others assumed they were going to die sooner or later and went into battle with an almost careless disregard over their fate. Their death was simply a matter of when and where, not if. One soldier explained that "Only then can he function as he ought to function under fire. He knows and accepts beforehand that he is dead, although he may still be walking around for a while."[29]

To push the perils of combat further from consciousness, infantrymen considered what they did as a job. After awakening, instead of heading to the factory or office, they stepped to the battlefield and put in a full day's work. A soldier who killed his first German during the fighting in the Hurtgen Forest along the German-Belgian border felt little guilt over the matter. He wrote, "I could stand there and watch him die and feel absolutely no qualms of any kind. . . . It was as if I were a carpenter and had driven home a nail which secured one beam to another, the job I was assigned to do."[30]

✯ Chapter 3 ✯

"They Stay and Fight"

Once a seaward invasion had succeeded and soldiers secured the beachhead, the next step was to move inland and seize cities and territory from the Germans. The American military hoped to hit the enemy often enough and hard enough to disrupt their organization and send them reeling back toward Germany. To do this, they had to wrest control of hundreds of villages, towns, and cities occupied by the German Army.

San Pietro

The small village of San Pietro in 1943 could have been selected by a tourist bureau as representative of hundreds of Italian villages. Quietly nestled along the rocky slopes of Monte Sammucro in the Apennine Mountains between Naples and Rome, the town's stone houses provided shelter for a thousand residents, who forged harsh lives harvesting olive trees and other farm products. World events normally rushed by the tiny place, but in late 1943 the U.S. and German armies shattered its peaceful existence.

San Pietro offered little of significance to the U.S. Army as it battled its way up the Italian peninsula toward Rome. The town simply stood in its path and offered shelter to hidden German infantry.

The Americans realized that taking San Pietro would not be easy. Any attack would have to start from the foot of Monte Sammucro and head up to the village. While the Americans would be exposed to German fire, their enemy would enjoy the protection provided by each stone house and by thick vegetation which grew along the few narrow trails that wound into the town. American soldiers would have to first fight their way in, then cautiously clear out each home before they could declare San Pietro secure.

In hopes of achieving surprise in the dark, two American battalions of about seven hundred men moved forward on the night of December 7, 1943. They quietly advanced along the slopes until sighting

American soldiers advance through rocky slopes toward San Pietro. U.S. troops could not rely on support from tanks due to the mountainous terrain.

the entrance to the village, at which time a withering curtain of German mortar shells, machine-gun fire, and artillery drove them back. Elsewhere in Europe, soldiers could call on tanks for support, but because of the rocky terrain and the numerous streams dissecting the area, the heavy vehicles could not be used in the village.

For eight days the Americans tried to hammer an entrance into San Pietro. Every attempt failed until December 15, when a force finally punctured a path into the town. The Americans then used the "fire and movement" tactic to neutralize each home. While some soldiers laid down a blanket of fire to pin down the Germans, others charged toward the objective. The first soldier arriving at the house fired into a window opening, then another tossed hand grenades through the same opening. As a third soldier advanced with a submachine gun and shot through the doorway, the first soldier leaped through the window opening to spray the interior with gunfire. Finally, the soldier at the door entered and added his firepower to the assault.

This dangerous maneuver, repeated until the last house fell, eventually removed the Germans from San Pietro. While the Americans lost more than 200 killed, over 1,000 wounded, and another 250 missing, the inhabitants of San Pietro suffered worse. During the fighting more than 30 percent of the town's inhabitants had died. In fact, the combating armies had so destroyed the town that the surviving residents had to rebuild on another location.

St. Lo

The French village of St. Lo offered a different challenge. Although once in the town American troops again relied on fire and movement to eliminate each strong point, the approach to thc town varied from that in San Pietro. To reach St. Lo, situated in northern France a short distance from the Normandy beaches, soldiers had to fight through hedgerows, towering banks of earth dating to Roman times. Six-foot hedgerows, sporting trees and bushes on top, surrounded each farmer's field. They were

Two residents of San Pietro sift through the remains of their village. Damage was so severe that survivors had to rebuild their town on another location.

used to keep cattle and to mark boundaries. Over the centuries the branches had grown to form a green canopy enclosing sunken roads that bordered each field. American soldiers could stand on one side of the thick foliage and not even see a German standing on the opposite side.

Americans entered a lethal green maze in July 1944 when they encountered hedgerow country. The Germans had presighted each field and every road so that wherever an American appeared, he faced fire or shells. To remove the enemy, Americans had to charge German machine-gun nests hidden in the hedgerows and remove them in hand-to-hand combat.

To cross a field, though, soldiers had to climb over the high hedgerows and attack through an exposed plot of land. One survivor mentioned that "Any soldier who could bring himself to leap over a hedgerow upon command and race, hunchbacked, across a grassy field while bullets snapped over his head like cracking whips, was a brave man indeed."[31]

Since this produced so many casualties, Americans experimented with different tactics, especially in coordination with tanks. The solution was to attach a hedgerow-cutting device to the front of tanks that enabled them to plow an opening through the obstacles. The tanks then fired white phosphorus—a painful substance that burns its way into the skin—into the opposite corners of the field and peppered the base of the hedgerow with machine-gun fire. A mortar

Protected by a tank, an American platoon advances through France. The tank is equipped with hedgerow cutters.

team lobbed shells onto suspected German positions while American infantry rushed through the gap and across to the other side.

The seemingly endless series of hedgerows that spread out before St. Lo exacted a heavy toll on American troops. One unit lost more men attacking St. Lo than they had at Omaha Beach. A medic dispensed so much morphine to wounded soldiers in the hedgerows that he nearly exhausted his supply.

The initial attack kicked off on July 11, which led to six days of intense combat. German bazookas knocked out a series of American tanks, and the only way to eliminate one group of Germans in an underground position was to have a bulldozer tank bury them alive. Once inside St. Lo, Americans had to carefully eliminate each house. Like San Pietro, the French village resembled an ancient ruin when the battle ended.

Heroes from Unexpected Sources

What makes men fight despite the tremendous fear that grips their bodies? Though scared and unprepared for such actions, for the most part American soldiers did their jobs throughout the fighting in Europe, whether it was on the beaches of Normandy or in an Italian village like San Pietro. One division commander said,

> About ten percent of a unit do all the fighting and will never cause you trouble—they are the backbone. About eighty percent are half-trained, scared to death, and waiting to see what someone else is going to do. The other ten percent never were and never will be any good.[32]

A tiny handful of men enjoyed war. Of all the soldiers wartime cartoonist Bill Mauldin encountered, only two seemed to relish the experience—a swamp hunter from Georgia and an exiled baron from Prussia. Mauldin explained that the swamp hunter loved to head out on his own to kill Germans and that the Prussian wanted to exact revenge for the financial loss suffered by his family because of the Nazis.

Most, however, fell into the category of those who saw the war as a job to be done, and these men could surprise people with their performance. One skinny Texan tried to join the marines, but the elite military outfit turned him down because of his low weight and fourth grade education. Barely heavy enough to join the army, the soldier received the nickname "Baby" from the rest of his unit because of his youthful appearance—he did not need to shave—and because he had once fainted during training. In southern France, however, he turned into a tiger on the battlefield and earned several medals, including the highest award that can be given, the Congressional Medal of Honor. The man, Audie Murphy, became the most decorated soldier in the nation's history.

The war boiled down to a series of individuals fighting little battles in small groups, rather than engaging the enemy as a large

To soldiers like Audie Murphy (pictured), accomplishing an objective was more important than personal safety.

army advancing in unison. When soldiers needed to take a hill or eliminate a bunker, for the moment that was the war. Nothing else mattered until the objective had been accomplished. As Audie Murphy explained, "I do not think of danger to myself. My whole being is concentrated on killing. . . . I remember the experience as I do a nightmare. A demon seems to have entered my body."[33]

Some soldiers fought because they did not want to appear cowardly to their buddies. This mutually supportive attitude kept some men from fleeing when they normally would head for cover. Robert Sherrod, a war correspondent, waded ashore with troops at different invasions, even when bullets were so thick that they seemed to pepper the water everywhere. When later asked why he kept walking toward shore, he answered, "Because that's what everyone else was doing. I'd have looked damned foolish if I had been the only one who turned and went the other way."[34]

Comradeship

The most important factor in pulling men through the horrors of combat was comradeship, having someone with whom they shared their experiences and emotions. Without a buddy, as they called each other, men felt isolated and vulnerable. But platoons consisting of men of varied backgrounds forged tight bonds because of the danger that they faced together.

The men shared problems from home. Audie Murphy described the time a man in his unit received a letter from his ten-year-old daughter asking permission to cut off her pigtails. The soldier read the letter to his buddies, and they engaged in a heated debate over what advice he should send home.

Historian S. L. A. Marshall claimed that a combat infantryman "is sustained by his fellows primarily and by his weapons secondarily. Having to make a choice in the face of the enemy, he would rather be unarmed and with comrades around him than altogether alone, though possessing the most perfect of quick-firing weapons."[35]

With his buddies, a man even had someone with whom he could die. One soldier recounted that if he was to be killed in France, at least it would happen "by T. L.'s side, surrounded by Berkely, the Arab, Duquesne, Casey, Gruening and the other stalwarts of the platoon."[36]

"You Don't Become a Killer"

In the heat of battle, infantrymen frequently did things they never would have considered doing back home. Grady Arrington claimed that in one day's combat in France he trespassed, lied, cheated, stole, and killed. Soldiers learned that when the struggle boiled down to kill or be killed, they forgot the niceties and did anything necessary to survive. Bill Mauldin stated that in combat, anything was proper. "You shoot him in the back, you blow him apart with mines, you kill or maim him the quickest and most effective way you can with the least danger

The Importance of a Comrade

S. L. A. Marshall was one of the nation's foremost experts on military history. In World War II he interviewed numerous soldiers to unearth their views on different issues. One area he researched was the issue of friendship during war. In his classic book about war, *Men Against Fire,* he explains the importance to soldiers of having a buddy.

I hold it to be one of the simplest truths of war that the thing which enables an infantry soldier to keep going with his weapons is the near presence or the presumed presence of a comrade. The warmth which derives from human companionship is as essential to his employment of the arms with which he fights as is the finger with which he pulls a trigger or the eye with which he aligns his sights. The other man may be almost beyond hailing or seeing distance, but he must be there somewhere within a man's consciousness or the onset of demoralization is almost immediate and very quickly the mind begins to despair or turns to thoughts of escape. In this condition he is no longer a fighting individual, and though he holds to his weapon, it is little better than a club.

Two infantrymen come under fire at the front. Having a comrade nearby was essential if a soldier was to be effective in combat.

An American soldier looks upon the body of a German he has killed in battle. In combat, men did things that they would never consider doing in civilian life.

to yourself. He does the same to you. He tricks you and cheats you, and if you don't beat him at his own game you don't live to appreciate your own nobleness."[37]

Mauldin added that, while the men fought a barbaric war in barbaric fashion, once it ended the same men would revert to their normal selves. He explained,

> You don't become a killer. No normal man who has smelled and associated with death ever wants to see any more of it. In fact, the only men who are even going to want to bloody noses in a fist fight after this war will be those who want people to think they were tough combat men, when they weren't. The surest way to become a pacifist is to join the infantry.[38]

Little Hope

Soldiers in Europe expressed a common gripe: They had little hope of soon returning home. Whereas combatants in other armies fought on the front lines and then were replaced, the American remained in combat. That Italian village he took on Wednesday turned into another village on Thursday. If he overran one hill, another loomed. He rushed one stone house in France knowing that hundreds more waited.

Though they clung to the thought of eventually returning home, most men stared at one of three options—death, injury, or capture. The 29th Division, which fought at Normandy, had a saying that their unit actually encompassed three separate divisions, one fighting at the front, one in the hospital, and another in the grave.

Even General Omar Bradley, a top European commander and one of the most popular officers from the fighting man's point of view, admitted the near hopelessness that most infantrymen felt.

> The rifleman fights without the promise of either reward or relief. Behind every river there's another hill—and behind that hill, another river. After weeks or months in the line only a wound can of-

fer him the comfort of safety, shelter and a bed. Those who are left to fight, fight on, evading death, but knowing each day of evasion they have exhausted one more chance of survival. Sooner or later, unless victory comes, this chase must end on the litter or in the grave.[39]

Soldiers grew weary of facing an indeterminate future on the front. One American infantryman wrote from Italy, "They send you to Tunisia, and then they send you to Sicily, and they send you to Italy. God knows where they'll send you after that. Maybe we'll be in France next year. . . . Then we work our way east. Yugoslavia. Greece. . . . All I know is, in 1958, we're going to be fighting the Battle of Tibet."[40]

As Italian villagers look on, a wounded soldier receives treatment from a medic. Death, injury, or capture were constant threats faced by American troops in Europe.

The truly heroic feature of soldiers in Europe was not so much that they courageously attacked position after position but that, despite the desire to be back home and despite the hopelessness, they continued to fight. Bill Mauldin sensed this. "They wish to hell they were someplace else, and they wish to hell they would get relief. They wish to hell the mud was dry and they wish to hell their coffee was hot. They want to go home. But they stay in their wet holes and fight, and then they climb out and crawl through minefields and fight some more."[41]

Somebody Didn't Deliver

While soldiers forged a strong bond with their buddies, they often found fault with American society. They believed the people in the United States were out of touch with reality and that they did not pull their fair share. Existing in comfortable conditions back home, the people knew little about what war was truly like, and did not seem to care at times. They enjoyed a booming wartime economy. Plentiful jobs offered high wages, and even though they might have to work long hours, they returned to cozy homes and beds each night. Soldiers shuddered when someone back home complained of a shortage of supplies, because they knew how much the home folks had.

The July 1943 issue of *Life* magazine published photographs of army training methods explaining how a soldier could use his thumbs to gouge out an enemy's eyes or use rifle butts to shatter jaws. Hundreds of protesting letters about the barbaric behavior poured into *Life*'s offices. Other pictures of American dead shocked people back home. When soldiers at the front read about this naive reaction, they shook their heads in amazement. What did they think occurred at the front?

A soldier who frequently entered combat against the Germans in France wondered,

> When they [civilians] hear about an airstrip being taken or a piece of land taken, they are happy, and they should be, but I often wonder if they stop to think there have been a lot of boys blown all apart and killed and lost arms and legs and eyesight and a lot more I'm not even going to mention.[42]

Poor work quality back home angered the frontline soldier. Weapons had to function as expected or the soldier might pay for it with his life. No matter how careful a worker in an American factory might be, the odds were that, out of hundreds of pieces of equipment, a few would malfunction. When they did, the soldier blamed the production worker. One gun crew in Italy spotted in time that the charge for a shell contained half the necessary powder to fire it. Had they inserted the charge, the smaller amount of powder would have propelled the shell right on top of an American gun crew directly in front. Instead of realizing that errors happen, soldiers griped that the workers were probably moaning about coffee shortages or how to spend their inflated wages.

The most detested of all actions on the home front was a labor strike. To men in a foxhole, surrounded by death, nothing was more irritating than knowing that other men their age who were fortunate enough to have avoided the draft actually withheld their work for higher pay.

One soldier wrote to his mother about the issue in no uncertain terms.

> That just burns me up when I think of those workers getting paid enormous

He Had No Feet

Soldiers had to make themselves immune to sights and sounds they normally could never stomach. John Ellis included the following description in his book about combat titled *The Sharp End.*

> One shell burst not 25 yards ahead of the Major [Johns]. . . . He ran forward into the smoke and dust, nearly falling over a man who was rolling crazily, half in and half out of the ditch. Johns grabbed him by the arm to help him to his feet, crying, "Come on, boy, let's go." The man tried to get up but stumbled awkwardly forward. Only then did Johns look down to see that the soldier had no feet. He was trying valiantly to stand on the stumps of his two legs, where his feet had been sliced cleanly off just at the ankles.

Artillery pieces undergo inspection in a factory. Soldiers blamed production workers back home when weapons failed to work properly.

wartime wages, getting all the work they want, plenty of food, clothes, and shelter, and still they are not willing to cooperate to keep the production and assembly lines moving. I would like for those discontented workers to be with us for a while on the front lines. Let them do without a decent meal for a month or so, let them wear the same clothes for weeks, let them spend a night or two in pouring rain without shelter. Every time they go on strike, they are not only slowing up production, but maybe they are actually costing the lives of those who have gone forth to protect them.[43]

Soldiers also hated reading in hometown papers that the sector in which they fought was "quiet" or that it saw what was described as "light action." They took it almost as an insult. First of all, there rarely were any quiet days. Second, when there were, the soldiers believed they deserved any moment of calm they received. As Bill Mauldin wrote,

> To a soldier in a hole, nothing is bigger or more vital to him than the war which is going on in the immediate vicinity of his hole. If nothing is happening to him, and he is able to relax that day, then it is a good war, no matter what is going on elsewhere. But if things are rough, and he is sweating out a mortar barrage, and his best friend is killed on patrol, then it is a rough war for him, and he does not consider it "comparatively quiet."[44]

Though these feelings commonly existed, the frontline soldier erred in thinking that the entire home front felt and behaved in this manner. Most people in the United States did sacrifice to some degree, and many understood as much as they could and appreciated what the soldiers at the front were doing.

What a Patrol!

Opposing troops often infiltrated the enemy's perimeter on nightly patrols to learn information about their foe or to seize some prisoners for interrogation. Sometimes, the patrols practically bumped into each other, as Sergeant James Pemberton explains in Stephen Ambrose's *Citizen Soldiers.* Pemberton led nine men into German lines, scouted about for a while, then started to return. As the column neared American lines, Pemberton counted his men.

> I had a problem, but I said nothing because I thought I knew what was going on and couldn't do anything about it. As soon as we got back to headquarters and into a lighted room I had my rifle ready and that [German] started yelling, "Kamerad, Kamerad!" No weapons or anything. He'd been on guard duty, heard us, and decided he'd had enough of the war and just joined my squad and became a POW [prisoner of war].

While the soldiers clashed with Germans in Italy or France, they simultaneously battled enemies that often confounded them, frequently frustrated them, and always made life more unbearable—terrain and weather.

★ Chapter 4 ★

Fighting Other Enemies

Although every soldier did not see combat, each American who served on the European mainland was affected by the weather and terrain. Enemy shells might not have posed a threat to some military units, but cold winters, driving rain, mud, dense forests, and lofty mountains plagued everyone. As usual, the infantrymen experienced the worst, for they not only had to live in horrid conditions, they had to fight and die in them.

Weather

Weather conditions varied according to where the soldier was. Surprisingly, much of the fighting in North Africa was not done under unbearably hot conditions because the main assaults occurred during winter months. Most men were astonished at the mild North African days and cold nights.

As American troops advanced through Sicily and onto the Italian peninsula, they battled temperatures approaching ninety degrees in the summer and thirty to fifty degrees in the winter, when cold drizzle drenched the troops and turned mountain passes into muddy quagmires. Since the early fighting in France occurred from June to September of 1944, fairly mild temperatures were the norm. As the armies pushed into Germany, however, snow and cold relentlessly hammered at them. The winter of 1944 proved to be one of the harshest ever recorded in Europe.

Mountain Terrain

To push the Germans out of Italy, Americans had to contend with the mountains that covered much of the peninsula. They had no choice but to attack one hill or mountain, fight up and over it, then assault the next one. According to the commanding officer of American troops in Italy, General Mark Clark, "Each hillside became a small but difficult military problem that could be solved only by careful preparation and almost inevitably by the spilling of blood."[45]

Battling against the cold, soldiers line up for food. The winter of 1944 was one of the most severe in European history.

Men fought in smaller units because of the mountainous peaks and plunging valleys. Frequently isolated even from their own officers, soldiers engaged in hand-to-hand combat with an enemy determined to halt their advance. One American unit might be only five hundred yards from another, but in the rocky, slippery terrain it would take hours to meet.

The mountains added their own deadly touch to warfare. Bombs exploding in the soil propelled thousands of tiny rock particles, each of which could kill. The sounds of explosions echoed in the mountain valleys, so each soldier felt he was under a constant barrage. Since supplying the troops along the narrow mountain trails was so difficult, hot food became a rarity and evacuation of wounded a torment.

The mountains unrolled in an unending dreary procession. Major General Fred L. Walker, commanding officer of the 36th Infantry Division, wrote in his diary that "taking one mountain mass after another gains no tactical advantage. There is always another mountain mass beyond with Germans on it."[46]

Sleep was difficult in the mountains. The cold drizzle soaked through uniforms to drench each man in a frigid coating. Men sought dips and hollows for protection from the wind and huddled close to each other for warmth. One soldier in Italy wrote to his parents, the rain "pinged and ticked off helmets, speckled the face and bare neck with cold. It came on steadily, and a transparent sheathing of ice began to loosen and fall from trees. Wet to the skin, the body shivered without pause; lips trembled."[47]

Constant rain turned dirt into mud, which halted vehicles, clogged rifles, sucked at boots, blackened faces and arms, and caused foot disease. Weary from fitful nights' sleeps because of the rain, soldiers lost their battle to keep dry and warm. Bill Mauldin described the Italian mud as a curse that made an intolerable situation worse.

A writer for *Yank* magazine described the conditions.

> Most of the time, for the men who are really up there, the war is a tough and dirty life, without immediate compensation. It is cold nights and no sleep, the beard matted on your face and the sores coming out on your feet, the clothes stiffening and the dirt caking on your body. It is digging and crawling and sweating out the 88s, inching forward over rocks and through rivers

Two tanks struggle through muddy terrain. Mud trapped vehicles, clogged weapons, caused disease, and made life even more miserable for soldiers.

to mountains that no one in his right mind would ever want. It is doing the same filthy job day after day with a kind of purposeless insanity; and dreaming all the time of warm beds with clean sheets and a steak the size of your arm; and pushing, always pushing.[48]

River Crossings

Since rivers and streams dissected the Italian peninsula and guarded the approach to Germany from France, American soldiers had to cross the natural obstacles many times on their march toward victory. A beautiful piece of landscape in peacetime turned deadly in war, for little was more dangerous than floating on water in front of enemy guns.

The endeavor required careful planning, because a normal river crossing took place against an enemy aiming guns and mortars from higher ground. Americans moved slowly in the rapid waters and thus became easy targets for German gunners. Once they landed on the other shore, they had to fight against a waiting enemy until the area was secured. In effect, American troops faced a miniature Omaha Beach every time they stared at a river.

Doctrine called for attackers to cross on floating assault boats or to traverse treacherous footbridges hurriedly installed by engineers as the fighting unfolded. Once across, the first troops were to remove the enemy from the shore so that engineers could erect a stronger bridge on which heavier equipment and more soldiers could flow.

The Rapido River between Rome and Naples in Italy provides an example. Steep banks three to six feet high enclosed a stream that varied in width from twenty-five to fifty feet and in depth from nine to twelve feet. The Germans fortified likely crossing points with machine-gun and mortar positions, trenches, and concrete bunkers sheltered by barbed wire and mines. On the river's opposite bank, where American soldiers would launch their attack, Germans planted hundreds of land mines.

To minimize casualties, the commanding officer hoped to achieve surprise with a night assault. On January 17, 1944, engineers cleared mines from the eastern bank across from the village of Sant'Angelo and marked safe zones with tape for the attacking soldiers to follow. As men appeared on the eastern bank, heavy German fire crossed the Rapido, disrupted operations, and erased much of the tape laid down by the engineers.

The Americans rushed to the river amid German bullets and land mines. Once in the river they either hopped into inflatable boats or cautiously stepped along the narrow footbridge erected shortly after the attack began. In either case, they were dangerously exposed to German fire until they reached the far side. Only a few men survived the deadly river crossing.

Subsequent attacks succeeded in dislodging the enemy, but the soldiers did not view their accomplishment as a triumph.

When crossing a river, troops first used footbridges or boats (left). Later, engineers constructed stronger bridges for use by tanks and heavy equipment (right).

Another river crossing beckoned, if not tomorrow, then the next day or week.

The Hurtgen Forest

While soldiers in Italy battled mountains and mud, rivers and rain, Americans nearing Germany faced another natural obstacle—the almost-impassable Hurtgen Forest. Situated south of Aachen along the German-Belgian border, the thick foliage of the Hurtgen Forest stretched for fifty square miles. Soldiers who entered had to push aside branches and weave through thousands of trees to advance a short distance, and anyone venturing without a compass stood a good chance of losing his way. The trees so completely blocked out the sun that a soldier felt he was walking in an unreal world.

As in the French hedgerow country, German and American soldiers could walk within yards of each other without realizing it. And similar to the combat in the Italian mountains, fighting in the Hurtgen Forest usually occurred among groups of about ten men, because larger numbers could not advance together in the thick woods.

Because tanks could rarely operate in the thick foliage, infantrymen engaged the enemy with their own rifles and grenades. A firefight could occur at any time, since

Captain Waskow

Ernie Pyle, the reporter most beloved by infantrymen, wrote a famous article in which he described one officer's death and the effect it had on the men he commanded. The article is included in a collection of Pyle's reporting edited by David Nichols called *Ernie's War.* Portions of the article appear below.

> In this war I have known a lot of officers who were loved and respected by the soldiers under them. But never have I crossed the trail of any man as beloved as Capt. Henry T. Waskow of Belton, Texas.
>
> Capt. Waskow was a company commander in the 36th Division. He had led his company since long before it left the States. He was very young, only in his mid-twenties, but he carried in him a sincerity and gentleness that made people want to be guided by him.
>
> "After my own father, he came next," a sergeant told me.
>
> "He always looked after us," a soldier said. "He'd go to bat for us every time."
>
> "I've never knowed him to do anything unfair," another one said.
>
> I was at the foot of the mule trail the night they brought Capt. Waskow's body down. . . . One soldier came and looked down, and he said out loud, "God damn it." That's all he said, and then he walked away.
>
> Another man came; I think he was an officer . . . and he reached down and took the dead hand, and he sat there for a full five minutes, holding the dead hand in his own and looking intently into the dead face, and he never uttered a sound all the time he sat there.
>
> And finally he put the hand down, and then reached up and gently straightened the points of the captain's shirt collar, and then he sort of rearranged the tattered edges of his uniform around the wound. And then he got up and walked away down the road in the moonlight, all alone.

each clump of trees could house enemy soldiers. The Germans used shells that exploded on contact with treetops and showered troops below with metal fragments and wood splinters. The normal procedure of falling to the ground when under artillery fire proved useless in the Hurtgen Forest. Instead, soldiers hugged trees so that only their helmets were exposed to the deadly particles shooting down.

The Battle of the Hurtgen Forest lasted for ninety days in late 1944 and produced carnage equal to D day. Americans suffered more than twenty-four thousand combat casualties, and another nine thousand were lost to disease or combat exhaustion. Private Clarence Blakeslee said, "The days were so terrible that I would pray for darkness, and the nights were so bad I would pray for daylight."[49]

The Battle of the Bulge

One of the war's biggest operations took place in December 1944, when Adolf Hitler hurled a potent offensive at the American troops along the French-German-Belgian border in hopes of puncturing a hole in their lines. Hitler hoped that the desperate winter scheme would so unnerve his foes that they would agree to halt the war.

Hitler selected a forested plateau called the Ardennes as his avenue of attack. His troops would smash through unprepared American lines, swing around behind them, and eliminate pockets of resistance. He planned on the frigid temperatures and snow to lessen American vigilance, for no one expected an attack in such conditions.

The attack commenced on December 16. German units quickly overran their surprised opponent and advanced near the French border. Soldiers on both sides fought through bitter winds, ankle-deep snow, and subzero temperatures that froze tank turrets and stalled vehicles.

The campaign's outcome hinged on the 101st Airborne Division near the Belgian town of Bastogne. Though German troops surrounded the Americans, the

German soldiers advance past abandoned American artillery during the Battle of the Bulge. Hitler hoped that the offensive would end the war in Europe.

101st refused to surrender. Battling the weather and running out of supplies, the Americans held on until help finally arrived a week later and turned back the German offensive.

The weather was almost their undoing. Dense fog prevented American aircraft from dropping supplies to the trapped men, and the temperatures plunged to deadly levels. Snows so densely blanketed the trees that if a soldier accidentally knocked against one too hard, he would be buried with snow. Men stuffed pine needles into empty tin ration cans, added gasoline, and lit them for warmth. At nighttime, when they could not afford to expose their position by lighting a fire, men paired up in their foxholes and slept in a womb position.

One soldier recalled, "The cold was enough of an adversary without the Germans. Just staying alive took all of one's ingenuity. I remember being on outpost right in front of the German lines where the choice seemed to be between moving and being shot, or lying perfectly still and freezing to death."[50]

A Segregated Army

While soldiers battled Germans, weather, and terrain, two groups faced an additional enemy that made their time in service more difficult. African-American and female soldiers discovered that, while they were in a war to preserve democracy, they often had to battle their own army even harder to gain rights enjoyed by their white, male counterparts.

Many positions behind the lines were filled by African Americans, not because of choice but because of an army policy of segregation. Like much of American society, the army carefully separated blacks and whites into their own units. "The world's greatest democracy fought the world's greatest racist [Hitler] with a segregated Army,"[51] claimed historian Stephen Ambrose.

Some white officers and soldiers believed that African Americans lacked both the intelligence to follow orders in combat and the skills to handle anything much beyond supply. The typical attitude was expressed by an army historian who wrote,

> If one phrase could summarize the Army's attitude toward blacks, it might well be "You know how niggers are." These words prefaced explanations by white officers that blacks could not be believed, that they had to be cursed at and hounded, and that they were oblivious to racial slurs, "nigger" for one. Many white officers did not credit blacks with intelligence, let alone hopes or ambitions or indeed feelings of any sort.[52]

Because of this, black units were commanded by white officers. Although the African Americans ably carried out their duties in a supporting role, until the latter part of the war they received little chance to prove that they could lead as well as fight.

"Just Plain Americans"

While African Americans battled the Germans on the front line, they struggled with bigotry and hatred behind it. Many white Americans considered blacks inferior, even though they had little objection to blacks' shedding their blood, ironically, in a fight for democracy. In his book about combat, *The Deadly Brotherhood,* historian John C. McManus cited the following quote from an African-American soldier named Joseph Johnson.

> Even as a soldier fighting . . . I'm denied many of the privileges as a Negro, to which the guys who wear the swastika are welcomed. Negroes are doing their bit here, their supreme bit, not for glory, not for honor but for, I think, the generation that will come. If the blood that flows here on Italy's mountains will wash from some folk's mind the stigma that has been bred there for years, then I think that the men who have gone so bravely here will not have given their lives in vain. I'm proud to be one of these few men who are fighters. The American papers call us "Tan yanks" and other fancy names, but . . . the Italians call us "Americans," just plain Americans. That's all we want to be, and one day I hope we will be just plain Americans.

Two African Americans pose with shells marked with messages to Hitler. Blacks had to fight against Germans as well as bigotry from their fellow countrymen.

Their introduction to army life could hardly have been reassuring since most of the training occurred in bases located in the Deep South, where weather conditions enabled the army to train during the entire year. There, the black soldiers encountered hostile whites, ranging from the local drugstore owner to the town sheriff. Alabama state police shot at black soldiers; rednecks harassed them; white soldiers picked fights.

The most shocking indignity may have been the treatment of African-American soldiers and German prisoners of war. In most southern towns, the white German captives enjoyed freedoms that were denied to blacks. Dempsey Travis stated,

> The army was an experience unlike anything I've had in my life. I think of two armies, one black, one white. I saw German prisoners free to move around the camp, unlike black soldiers, who were restricted. The Germans walked right into the doggone places like any white American. We were wearin' the same uniform, but we were excluded.[53]

Once overseas, African-American troops were excluded from many army assignments because the military leadership believed that blacks and whites could not work together as a team. Thus three out of every four black soldiers served in a support unit, such as communications, engineering, or the Quartermaster Corps. Most landing craft on D day were driven by black soldiers, and black soldiers formed the core of those working for the important Red Ball Express trucks that transported supplies to the front. Only 5 percent ever served in the infantry, and that occurred much later in the war.

Blacks were finally used in the infantry in late 1944 when the army faced a serious manpower shortage. The high number of casualties, combined with the erroneous belief that the nation could decrease the number of men it drafted, created such shortages that units at the front were badly undermanned. One way to quickly reinforce the front lines was to send black units into combat. Although African Americans now shared the same

Two black soldiers and their white commander stand over a dead German storm trooper.

What Are We Fighting For?

The irony of African-American soldiers fighting for freedom when American society denied them many basic rights is articulately conveyed in the following letter. Written by Corporal Rupert Trimmingham to *Yank* magazine, it recounts a disturbing episode and asks some basic questions. The letter was reprinted in the 1945 book *The Best from* Yank, *the Army Weekly.*

> Here is a question that each Negro soldier is asking. What is the Negro soldier fighting for? On whose team are we playing? Myself and eight other soldiers were on our way from Camp Claiborne, La., to the hospital here at Fort Huachuca. We had to lay over until the next day for our train. On the next day we could not purchase a cup of coffee at any of the lunchrooms around there. As you know, Old Man Jim Crow [the name given to segregation] rules. The only place where we could be served was at the lunchroom at the railroad station but, of course, we had to go into the kitchen [to eat]. But that's not all; 11:30 a.m. about two dozen German prisoners of war, with two American guards, came to the station. They entered the lunchroom, sat at the tables, had their meals served, talked, smoked, in fact had quite a swell time. I stood on the outside looking on, and I could not help but ask myself these questions: Are these men sworn enemies of this country? Are they not taught to hate and destroy . . . all democratic governments? Are we not American soldiers, sworn to fight for and die if need be for this, our country? Then why are they treated better than we are? Why are we pushed around like cattle? If we are fighting for the same thing, if we are to die for our country, then why does the Government allow such things to go on?

dangers as white combat soldiers, they still served in their own units.

One unit whose performance garnered attention was the all-black 761st Tank Battalion. The unit so excelled in training that General George S. Patton requested it for his dash across France. When the battalion joined his forces in October 1944 and became the first black unit assigned to combat, Patton told them,

> Men, you're the first Negro tankers to ever fight in the American army. . . . I don't care what color you are, as long as you go up there and kill those [Germans]. Everyone has their eyes on you and is expecting great things from you. Most of all, your race is looking to you. Don't let them down, don't let me down.[54]

Blacks slowly entered other areas previously closed to them. Half the field artillery battalions during the December Battle of the Bulge were black, and in March 1945 thirty-seven black rifle platoons entered the front lines.

When some white soldiers saw African Americans perform well in combat, their attitudes started to change. One white officer who was impressed by the performance of the black soldiers he commanded in

France sent a message to those who believed that race mattered. "Maybe if people just didn't worry about us being something special. Maybe if somebody could come up here and see how we've been fighting and killing and dying, how it doesn't seem to matter a damn what your color is."[55]

The front dissolved racial stereotypes held by some whites and brought people closer together. Other white soldiers, trapped in the bitterness of bigotry, attributed exemplary battlefield conduct by African Americans to weak opposition or luck.

While much remained to be accomplished before African-American soldiers attained equality (many Red Cross clubs preferred that black troops stay away, and the Red Cross even separated blood donated by blacks to ensure that no white received a transfusion) infant steps had been taken. Within ten years of the war's end, the army would be integrated.

Women in Uniform

The other group excluded from full equality in the army were women. A Women's Auxiliary Army Corps had been established in 1942, but the organization was not formally a part of the army. Formal recognition came in June 1943 with the establishment of the Women's Army Corps (WAC). Nearly ten thousand women served in Europe, mainly as medical technicians, military photographers stationed in headquarters, and clerks.

The women faced almost as much hostility as black troops. Many male soldiers labeled them hookers, lesbians, or sexually promiscuous individuals. They hated that women were considered soldiers just as frontline infantrymen were. Parents attempted to talk their daughters out of joining because of the notorious publicity, and brothers serving overseas wrote letters home warning their sisters about enlisting.

Sergeant Bob Bowie mailed a letter to *Yank* magazine expressing his frustration at allowing women into the military.

> Who in the hell cares about these dimpled GIs who are supposed to be soldiers? All I have ever heard of them doing is peeling spuds, clerking in the office, driving a truck or tractor or puttering around in a photo lab. . . . It's sickening to read about some doll who has made the supreme sacrifice of giving up her lace-trimmed undies for the ODs [Olive Drab uniforms].[56]

Though many male soldiers held the same views, female soldiers did not allow such comments to go unchallenged. Private Mildred McGlamery answered Bowie's letter by replying, "Hell hath no fury like a WAC criticized. . . . Many of these frilly females Sgt. Bowie blows his top about are a lot closer to action than a smug soldier who apparently has enough time to sit at his desk . . . and write letters critical of the WACs."[57]

Although some women gained admiration from the men serving alongside them, another group of female soldiers had a

Four WACs use a portrait of Hitler as a dartboard. While not directly participating in combat, women did serve in supporting roles.

tougher time—African-American women. Four thousand African-American women joined the WACs, but they had to live in separate barracks, eat at their own tables, and perform menial tasks such as mopping floors and doing the laundry. Almost five hundred black women served as nurses, but they were sadly relegated to caring for German prisoners of war because military authorities did not consider it socially proper to have a black nurse tend a white soldier.

★ Chapter 5 ★

Support from the Military and from Home

One portion of the European fighting produced a type of warfare that had not been seen on the mainland since German troops rushed across Poland in 1939. In the summer of 1944 American tanks and infantry, after battling out of Normandy, sped through the French countryside in a mad race to reach the German border. In an impressive display of coordination among military departments, American infantry covered in days the territory it took months and years to seize in World War I. By the first week of October, elements of the U.S. Army stood along the Rhine River, nature's final obstacle protecting Germany.

Close Air Support

Much of the success came from the fertile mind of Major General Elwood Quesada. After watching the slow advance out of Normandy, he realized that artillery units, aircraft, and infantry had to maintain closer communications with each other. That way, when ground troops encountered stiff resistance, they could call in artillery and air support.

Quesada argued that radios should be installed in fighter aircraft and given to artillery units. Soldiers using similar radios in tanks advancing with the infantry could then call down fire on German defenders. By July, radiomen became so proficient in close air support (CAS) that they could bring aircraft bombing to within 350 yards of their position.

American dominance of the skies demoralized the Germans. Since their own air force either had been destroyed by American and British bombers or were being held back by Hitler to defend the homeland, few German aircraft rose to duel American fighters. Thus any significant gathering of German forces usually brought in fire. American aircraft, roaming the skies at will, spotted them and contacted artillery units on the ground, who poured on a devastating round of shells.

A formation of American fighters patrols the skies over Europe. Aircraft worked with ground troops and artillery units to destroy German strongholds and equipment.

The advance to the German border was "a wild, mad, exciting race to see which army [American or British] could gain the most ground in a single day,"[58] stated Lieutenant George Wilson of the 4th Infantry Division. In France, American units, especially the armored divisions of General George S. Patton's 3rd Army, captured tons of equipment and supplies from the fleeing enemy. In one location they seized 2.6 million pounds of frozen beef.

American infantry enacted the same procedure over and over as they sped toward Germany. They discovered a German position, they used the fire and movement tactic to eliminate it, then they moved on until another enemy concentration halted their drive. The work was dangerous, unglamorous, and necessary—it was the only way they could get the war over and head back home. One rifle platoon leader, Robert Jackson, said of his men as they moved toward Germany, "Looking back, I see what a well-trained unit we were. There was little panic and jobs were done to the best of our abilities under terrible circumstances. This was not the stuff of awards, but competent soldierly activity under the great stress of fear."[59]

Patrols were essential to the success of this rapid advance. Both sides constantly sent out small groups of men either to locate where enemy units stood or to capture an enemy soldier and bring him back for questioning. Few soldiers volunteered for the dangerous job, but all had to do their share. That share included taking a turn as point man—the lead man in the patrol who walked ahead of the others. One soldier explained that "A point man needs a willingness to die. He is nothing more . . . than a decoy. When he is shot, the enemy position is revealed. Don't confuse this willingness with 'bravery.' A point man is just doing his job, what he has trained to do."[60]

Many men darkened their faces and hands with mud to better disguise their features in the dark. They taped weapons, dog tags, and other items that might rattle, then headed away from their own lines and into enemy territory. They frequently moved so close to German soldiers that they could listen to their conversations.

Three soldiers hug the ground in search of the enemy. The point man probes the underbrush at the upper left of the photograph.

Advancing so close to the enemy resulted in either valuable information or a firefight. One patrol cautiously approached what appeared to be an abandoned farmhouse in Germany when suddenly the trees standing next to the house began to shake. A German tank, sheltered by the thick pine trees, opened fire. One man was killed and two others injured before the patrol made it back to its own lines.

Army Organization

The drive across France and the other military operations conducted in Europe could not have succeeded without organization. The U.S. Army is supremely organized. Each unit has its number, each soldier his job. The army had to be organized if it was to exert the greatest amount of pressure against Germany with the largest number of men and the most lethal concentration of firepower.

To manage the colossal numbers of personnel, the army placed men into different groups. In Europe, for instance, the U.S. 1st Army and U.S. 3rd Army advanced along different routes in their march toward Germany. Each army consisted of two to three units called corps. Each corps contained three divisions of fifteen to twenty thousand men commanded by a general. The corps headquarters was responsible for coordinating the divisions under its control and stood some distance behind the actual fighting.

Each division was further broken down into three regiments. Commanded by a colonel, whose regimental headquarters stood closer to the front, these units contained about five thousand men each. The five thousand men were placed into three battalions, led by a major, and the battalions were split into six companies under the supervision of a captain.

As an observer neared the front lines, he encountered the smaller units. Four platoons of about fifty men each were led by a lieutenant, normally in his early to mid-twenties. When the lieutenant required a smaller group of men to carry out a mission, he sent a squad, which consisted of a sergeant, a corporal, and ten privates.

At the Front

The territory known as the front varied, but it usually extended to the rear about a third of a mile. This was the domain of the fighting man. Though company command posts stood less than three hundred yards behind the front lines, riflemen considered them rear echelon troops. Private J. A. Craft typified the infantryman's viewpoint when he stated that the rear echelon was "any son of a bitch behind my foxhole."[61]

Soldiers along the front line lived a totally different existence from superior officers and support troops a short distance to the rear. The soldier dug a foxhole in which he and a buddy took refuge. The rectangular foxholes, dug each night or whenever a drive stalled, measured approximately three feet wide, six feet long, and four to five feet deep, although the size

As two infantrymen scan the forest for enemy activity, a third uses a field telephone to report their situation to a commanding officer.

greatly varied depending on the circumstances. The foxhole was meant to provide a minimum of shelter from enemy rifle and machine-gun fire and from exploding shells, which splattered hundreds of metallic pieces called shrapnel in every direction. If a soldier huddled in a foxhole below the ground surface, the bullets and shrapnel would normally miss him.

After digging the holes, soldiers secured the area by stretching wires attached to grenades across likely approaches, planting land mines, and running communications lines back to commanding officers. Thus, if the enemy attempted to approach during the night, he would alert the Americans by tripping a wire or stepping on a land mine. A speedy call would bring supporting artillery fire.

Extending dangerously toward the enemy were outposts. Sprinkled among the land mines and wired approaches, these outposts of two men stood guard ahead of the rest of their unit to give early warning. Every two hours, two other men cautiously crept forward to relieve them and continue the heart-stopping vigil. The outposts could be as far as fifty yards away from the main body of American soldiers or as close as ten, and frequently they stood within hearing distance of German outposts.

Lieutenant Lee Otts once slumped in a foxhole that actually stood nearer to the German line of foxholes than it did to American foxholes to his right and left. He eavesdropped on their conversations, and "They were so close we could hear the clink of the metal and the gurgle of the water as they filled their canteens."[62]

Sometimes men occupied their foxholes for long periods of time; other stretches lasted a day or so. When men existed in such conditions for any lengthy period of time, they emerged dark with filth and covered with grime. One soldier recalled that, when he was pulled out of the front line one time in France, "some of the green 69th Division troops passing by were convinced that they were relieving an all black infantry battalion."[63]

Artillery

The frontline soldier both loved and envied men in the artillery—those who handled the howitzers and big guns. He envied them because they operated more

Home Front Sacrifice

Infantrymen often wondered how much the people back home sacrificed for the war effort. They and their buddies risked their lives every day, but what about those who were not drafted? The soldiers' attitude on this matter is clearly expressed by this excerpt from Bill Mauldin's *Up Front*.

> The attitude of the dogface [soldier] toward America and the home front is a complex thing. Nobody loves his own land more than a soldier overseas, and nobody swears at it more. He loves it because he appreciates it after seeing the horrible mess that has been made of Europe. . . .
>
> He has seen the results of the German occupation of France and the fury of the French people and their savage revenge upon anything German. He has seen stark fear and utter destruction and horrible hunger. But at the same time he has seen families bravely trying to rebuild their shattered homes, and he has seen husbands and wives with rifles fighting ahead of him in France. He knows how they can throw themselves completely and unselfishly into the war when it is necessary.
>
> So he is naturally going to get sore when he thinks of selfishness at home. He got just as sore at the big company which was caught bribing inspectors and sending him faulty armor for his tanks as he did at the workers who held up production in vital factories. He doesn't have time to go into economics and labor-management problems. All he knows is that he is expected to make great sacrifices for little compensation, and he must make those sacrifices whether he likes it or not. Don't expect him to weigh the complicated problem before he gets sore. He knows he delivered and somebody else didn't.

A gun crew fires its weapon during a night action. When under attack, American soldiers counted on the artillery to pulverize enemy offensives.

than a thousand yards behind the front lines, which meant they enjoyed a safety and comfort level never attained by combat soldiers. However, in an attack, the soldiers counted artillerymen among their blessings, for in minutes these individuals could rain down a destructive curtain of artillery shells that broke up enemy offensives.

Artillerymen employed a fire direction center to coordinate their barrages. Each field artillery battalion established a communications center to handle the flow of information. The officer in charge selected the artillery targets based on this knowledge. Radio contact with forward observers at the front provided some of the information, while observers in small aircraft spotted the targets below.

Artillerymen operated on the principle called "On Time, On Target." Every gun within range would formulate their fire so that all shells would simultaneously hit the same target in a cataclysmic explosion. If the artillery officer had three targets and one hundred guns under his command, rather than split the three targets among his guns, he would train all one hundred guns on the target with top priority, knock it out, then move on to the second target.

Tanks

The mammoth, steel-plated fortresses rumbled into battle with a frightening noise, spit out shells and bullets in alarming numbers, and frequently wound up as coffins for the Americans inside. In most Hollywood films, tanks appear as indestructible weapons that offered safety and shelter to infantrymen, but in reality American tanks often provided neither.

German Panther and Tiger tanks were so superior to the American Sherman tank that one American commander claimed it took four Shermans to equal a Panther and eight to compare to the superb Tiger tank. Any engagement in which the numbers of tanks were equal ended in a German victory; only with overwhelming superiority in numbers and assistance from artillery could the Americans defeat a group of German tanks.

In one action, an American tank landed three hits on a Panther, but the frustrated tank commander watched them bounce harmlessly off the sturdier German vehicle. German soldiers had such little regard for American tanks that they compared them to a popular cigarette lighter of the day. "Ronson, you know. Ronsons, like for a cigarette," stated a German soldier. "Our gunners see your tanks coming . . . and they say to each other, 'Here

A dead German lies on the remains of his Tiger tank. Superior to the American Sherman tank, a Tiger could be defeated only when it was outnumbered and targeted by artillery.

comes another Ronson.' Why do the Americans do this for us? Bang! and it burns like twenty haystacks. All the people [inside], my God. . . . Why does the country . . . send their men out to die in these things?"[64]

Consequently, many frontline soldiers doubted the value of tank support. Though tanks could smash through German strongholds, Americans also knew that German artillery observers called for a barrage whenever they spotted an American tank.

Their greatest value came in the American dash across France, during which General George S. Patton's 3rd Army crashed through German lines and sped deep into enemy territory, causing a German retreat. Rather than supporting infantrymen, though, the tanks acted as a separate unit, similar to the cavalry of Wild West days.

An Army Air Corps pilot prepares for a mission. Unlike infantrymen, pilots fought in relatively comfortable conditions and knew when they could return to the United States.

Airmen

The group of servicemen that received the most jealousy from infantry was the Army Air Corps. Frontline soldiers watched fliers soar above the mud and slime on the way to their targets and knew that, once the mission was complete, they returned to comfortable bases in England, enjoyed a decent meal—sometimes in the company of a beautiful nurse—and slept in a bed with sheets. It was common knowledge that the Air Corps handed out more medals than did any other branch and that pilots received extra "flight" pay. On top of all this, the home front seemed mesmerized with the exploits of pilots while ignoring the daily struggles of the infantry.

What most upset the infantryman was that, for much of the war, the army rotated pilots home after they completed a certain number of missions. Whereas airmen could count down the missions until they left the fighting, the infantry knew they would return home only when the war ended.

This resentment toward pilots ignored the fact that, after the infantry, airmen suffered the highest rate of casualties in the military. And when combat soldiers needed fliers to support an advance or to wipe out a German machine gun, they could so unfailingly count on them that they labeled fighter pilots the "angels on their shoulders."

Farther behind the lines, the Red Cross set up small cafes or recreation centers where soldiers could enjoy coffee and doughnuts. In some ways the Red Cross centers made the men feel as if they were back in the United States. One soldier compared them to "the one little spot of home . . . and the one touch of 'mother' you find when in trouble."[66]

Whenever conditions permitted, a company of men would be allowed to

"A Haven of Refuge"

To give the men a few moments of relaxation, most units established rest areas within a few miles of the front lines. Though the rest area may have only been a fortified bunker that offered hot coffee, as was set up on the Anzio beaches during the invasion of Italy, it at least offered a break from the blood and violence of the battlefield and a place to escape the cold or rain. As one infantryman said, "To a soldier on the verge of exhaustion, an opportunity to dry out in a safe place for a few hours is a haven of refuge that will revive his will to fight."[65]

Soldiers line up for a shower at a Red Cross center behind the lines in France. Troops often had to go for months without bathing or relaxation.

leave the front lines for a few days' rest. Soldiers anticipated these brief escapes from warfare with an intensity that sometimes produced strange results. One time a division was pulled out of the line and had an opportunity to take their first shower in two months. As the naked, weary men waited in line for their moment under warm water, a sergeant from division headquarters shouted, "All right, you guys, you got one minute to wet, one minute to soap, and one minute to rinse off and then you get out of here." A private quietly picked up his rifle, pointed it at the sergeant, who lived in relative comfort while the private and his buddies fought on the lines, and calmly asked, "Sergeant, how much time did you say we have?"[67] The sergeant backed down and gave the men extra time in the showers.

Entertainment at the Front

In an effort to sustain morale, the army provided different forms of entertainment for the troops. Even though top-name performers traveled to Europe and Hollywood made first-run movies available, the frontline soldier was often slighted. Because of the army's concern for the safety of top Hollywood stars, the performers usually entertained troops at some distance behind the front lines. Thus it was not combat soldiers but support staff and officers working in headquarters far from the fighting who enjoyed the shows.

The most popular entertainers were comedians Bob Hope and Joe E. Brown. Brown particularly earned the appreciation of combat soldiers because he insisted on visiting the front lines. Another entertainer who earned their approval was singer Frank Sinatra. Though most soldiers were jealous at first because most females back home were crazy for him, Sinatra won over the men by crooning tender, romantic ballads.

Motion pictures were also shown to soldiers. During the fighting in Italy, movies were shown twice a day within shooting range of the front lines. In France and elsewhere, improvised movie theaters sprang up in hospitals, rear echelon centers, and rest areas. Comedians Bud Abbott and Lou Costello proved huge favorites, as were starlets such as Betty Grable, Rita Hayworth, and Ginger Rogers.

In a 1944 *Time* magazine poll, soldiers indicated that they preferred musical comedies best, followed by comedies, adventure films, then dramas. One general concluded that movies were as vital as food and supplies, and General Dwight D. Eisenhower, who commanded all forces landing on D day, ordered that movies be made abundant to the troops.

Soldiers mocked some films as being unrealistic, simplistic in their portrayal of war, or too patriotic. Combat veterans especially howled at war films. They laughed when they watched John Wayne charge the enemy with his bayonet attached to his rifle, because they rarely, if ever, used such a device. Actors tossed grenades incorrectly, and all movies about the war ended with the hero saving the day. Soldiers scoffed when Wayne or Humphrey Bogart projected the tough guy image because they knew that nothing could be tougher than the combat they faced. John Wayne acted his toughness; the soldiers lived theirs.

Soldiers wanted lighthearted films rather than those that were filled with patriotic messages and stirring speeches. Films offered an escape, and they did not want Hollywood to ruin that by inserting wartime propaganda. Besides, they did not want any reminders of their grim reality. As one soldier put it, "Tell the movie bigs to cut out the corn about the grand old flag and the great sacrifice the boys are making. It's nauseating from where we sit, not because it isn't true, but why bring it up?"[68]

Mail

No matter where the soldier served, he always looked forward to receiving mail from home. Whether engaging the Germans in hedgerow territory, battling in the Italian mountains, or chasing the enemy across France, the American soldier always had time for mail. Though mail could not be regularly delivered because of the varying conditions at the front, infantrymen rarely went a week without mail arriving.

The army transported a huge volume of mail. In 1943 the typical soldier received fourteen pieces each week, and a survey of soldiers fighting in Italy indicated that more than half had written a letter in the previous twenty-four hours.

The Andrews Sisters Entertain

One of the most popular singing acts of the 1940s was a trio of sisters called the Andrews Sisters. Maxine, Patty, and Laverne visited hospitals throughout Europe to cast a bit of sunshine into the soldiers' lives and deliver a taste of home. However, near a San Francisco hospital, they learned that they could produce a powerful effect without leaving the United States. Maxine Andrews recalled the moment for Studs Terkel's moving collection of interviews, *The Good War.*

> When we were announced, there wasn't any applause at all. It was a very long ward. We were ushered into the middle. There were beds in front of us, beds behind us. We finally looked. The sight was terrible. We saw boys with no arms or legs, with half-faces. The three of us held on to each other, because we were afraid we were going to faint. . . .
>
> As we were leaving, a male nurse came over to us: "I have a young patient who would love to hear you sing." He asked us to sing something soft. Nice and easy and relaxed. We went down a long, long hallway and stopped in front of a door that two male nurses were guarding. We were ushered in. We were in a padded cell. The two guards closed the door behind us. We were alone.
>
> In the corner, we saw a figure facing the wall. We started to sing "Apple Blossom Time." About halfway through, we began to hear this hum. It was discordant and got louder and louder. When we came to the end of the song, we didn't stop. We just kept singing. We repeated it and repeated it. The figure turned around. He couldn't have been more than nineteen years old. His eyes were looking at us, but he wasn't seeing us. He was lost in another world. He was just humming and humming. He was so handsome and so young.

A soldier enjoys a letter from home. Even in combat situations, men rarely went a week without receiving mail.

Soldiers became angry and despondent if a mail call occurred and they received nothing. One recalled, "The mail had been sidetracked. We had no idea what was happening in the world outside. We had no outside. Psychologically it did something to me. I wrote a letter home: 'You've forsaken me. You don't write and I'm gonna die.'"[69]

The letters could bring pain as easily as comfort. If a wife, mother, or sweetheart wrote of some major problem, the soldier seethed in frustration over his inability to do anything. He could do nothing but worry, an attitude that was not conducive to careful behavior at the front. An army psychiatrist claimed that as many casualties were caused by disturbing mail as by enemy bullets.

The worst were the "Dear John" letters, letters sent by girlfriends or wives informing the soldier that she had found someone else and was breaking off their relationship. Sometimes, the one factor that kept a man going was the love of a wife or girlfriend, and if that was suddenly withdrawn, the consequences could be disastrous. Whenever it occurred, the man's buddies gathered around him, shared his pain, and let him know that his true home—his unit—would never let him down.

Another problem was that many soldiers wished to unburden themselves in their letters, but they could not share the horrors of the battlefield or the fear they felt. First of all, as one historian put it, no soldier was going to write, "Dear Mother, I am scared to death."[70] That would do nothing to help the infantryman and would cause great consternation back home. Consequently, little of substance about warfare entered their writing.

"I never let them know my true feelings," explained one soldier. "I could see no profit in such forthrightness, either way. Cut away and immune from the sickness of military life, [the people back home] could offer no remedy but their love, which I never doubted; yet meanwhile they would themselves suffer in sympathy, which I could not abide."[71]

Soldiers also shied away from describing what combat was like because they feared that people back home might think they were cowards. Soldiers at the front lines shiver from fright and huddle in fear, but how does one explain that to someone so distant from the action? One woman received such a letter from her soldier boyfriend.

> He was sent to Italy where the fighting was very intense for a long time, and he wrote to me whenever he could. Then, in one . . . he told me he cried many nights during the heavy fighting. In my sheltered life with my stereotyped notions of what [constituted] a man . . . the thought of his crying turned my stomach. I was convinced I had loved a coward. I never wrote to him again.[72]

Most soldiers simply believed it was futile to attempt to explain combat to a person who could never experience it. As Bill Mauldin explained,

> But no matter how much we try we can never give the folks at home any idea of what war really is. I guess you have to go through it to understand its horror. You can't understand it by reading magazines or newspapers or by looking at pictures or by going to newsreels. You have to smell it and feel it all around you until you can't imagine what it used to be like when you walked on a sidewalk or tossed clubs up into horse chestnut trees or fished for perch or when you did anything at all without a pack, a rifle, and a bunch of grenades.[73]

Ads Can Be Deceiving

Soldiers at the front generally believed that people back home did not have the slightest idea what they faced in combat or what they most wanted. In his book *Up Front,* Bill Mauldin explains the reaction to a magazine ad.

> I remember one lulu of a refrigerator ad showing a lovely, dreamy-eyed wife gazing across the blue seas and reflecting on how much she misses Jack . . . BUT she knows he'll never be content to come back to his cozy nest (equipped with a Frosty refrigerator; sorry, we're engaged in vital war production now) until the Hun is whipped and the world is clean for Jack's little son to grow up in.
>
> Chances are that Jack, after eighteen or twenty months of combat, is rolling his eyes and making gurgling sounds every time the company commander comes around, so the old man will think he is battle-happy and send him home on rotation. Like hell Jack doesn't want to come home now.

★ Chapter 6 ★

"Missions of Mercy"

The Geneva Convention of 1929 was an agreement signed by many nations that decided to adhere to a set of rules governing several aspects of behavior, including treatment of prisoners of war and the wounded on the battlefield. For instance, opposing nations were to provide medical assistance to wounded soldiers, even soldiers from the other side; they were to treat prisoners decently; and they were to allow medics and chaplains to tend to injured and dying men.

No formal method governed the acceptance of surrendering soldiers. Combatants were expected to kill each other during battle, but once an enemy lay down his arms, the fight supposedly ended and he became the prisoner of the other side. Generally the United States and Germany abided by this provision.

However, what was easily put on paper was not as readily enacted in the field. There were times when Americans refused to accept surrender. German snipers killed so many Americans on D day that one unit shot every one they came across. No matter how the fighting went or what stage the war was in, if Americans captured a diehard Nazi supporter or a member of Hitler's elite military unit called the SS, they did not take prisoners. Walter Rosenblum explained, "There were two kinds of Germans we captured: these kids and the SS troops. The SS were impossible. They thought they had won the war, even after we captured them. They were beyond belief. But the average German soldier was just a young man who was drafted."[74]

Consequently, many Americans figured that the regular German soldier was only doing his job. In one heated episode, an American intended to kill a surrendering German because he had just seen his buddy die, but other men from his unit stopped him by stating that "he's only a soldier like you and me. . . . [He] fought because he had to."[75]

A wounded German receives first aid from an American medic. Both sides were bound by the Geneva Convention to treat prisoners decently.

American soldiers sometimes hesitated to take German prisoners because they knew the destination that awaited the captive—incarceration in the United States. Infantrymen battled throughout the fall of 1944 and into 1945 dreaming of the day they could head home, so the thought of sending their opponent to a relatively comfortable prisoner of war camp in America while they had to continue fighting did not sit well. "The treatment of German prisoners in America was a sore point with us," wrote an American pilot who spent part of the war in a German prison camp. "Rumors that they were attending dances, given rations of beer, steak, ice cream, etc., made us seethe in envy."[76]

Germans reacted similarly to American captives. Americans quickly learned not be caught with a German item in their possession because the Germans assumed it must have come from a dead German soldier. The offending Americans were shot, and sometimes the Germans slashed huge "X"s across their chests as a warning to other Americans.

One of the worst atrocities committed against Americans took place on December 17, 1944, at Malmédy. About 150 American prisoners were gathered together in a field, then slaughtered by German soldiers armed with rifles and machine guns. Nearly seventy miraculously survived, but word of the incident embittered Americans on the front lines.

These incidents proved to be the exception, however. Most soldiers from both sides who surrendered wound up in prison camps, where they spent the remainder of the war. Conditions for American prisoners, though far from ideal, were at least civilized. Until the war's later stages, they had enough food to survive, sufficient warmth in their barracks, and relatively acceptable living conditions.

Dead American prisoners lie in a field at Malmédy after being slaughtered by their German captors.

"Special Rules of Conduct"

On many occasions, one side or the other allowed medics and chaplains to tend to the wounded and dying on the battlefield. Though men had to be on guard during these incidents, since it took only one enraged soldier to start firing at the medic, for the most part both sides acted with a sense of decency that never existed in the Pacific.

During an attack on one German position in November 1944, two American soldiers wounded from gunshots fell into barbed wire that was strung out between the two forces. An American private stood up in the heat of battle and waved a white flag to get the Germans' attention. An officer from each side cautiously stepped into the open and agreed to stop shooting until the wounded had been removed from the wire. While medics rushed to their assistance, German and American soldiers stood up, stretched their aching muscles, and walked about a bit. When the wounded were safely behind lines, everyone returned to their positions and resumed shooting.

On another occasion, in which German forces made rapid advances, doctors in an American aid station found themselves surrounded by the enemy. A German officer asked the physicians if they had enough supplies to treat the wounded, then posted a guard at the station to ensure that no other German unit bothered them.

An American soldier later described a typical arrangement.

Medics to the Rescue

The impact that unit medics made on soldiers is one of the most vivid memories infantrymen carry from battle. Cartoonist Bill Mauldin included this description in his riveting book about war *Up Front.*

> Let's say the doggie has a shattered leg and is lying in a shell hole out in front of his company, which is pinned down by machine-gun fire. He uses the bandage from his first-aid packet to make a tourniquet, and he takes the sulfa pills, but he knows that if he lies there much longer he will bleed to death.
>
> Nobody is going to blame the aid man if he saves his own neck and doesn't go out after a man who will probably die anyway. But the medic usually goes. If the Germans are feeling pretty good, they might lift their fire when they see his red-cross armband.
>
> Put yourself in the wounded guy's shoes when he sees the medic appear over him, and his pain is dulled by morphine, his bleeding is stopped, and he is lifted out and carried back to safety and good surgery. Sure, he's going to love that medic. And after a few dozen men owe their lives to one man, that little pill roller is going to be very well liked indeed.
>
> Sooner or later, like everybody who works around the infantry, the medic is going to get his. Many aid men have been wounded and many have been killed. It should comfort the families of those who have died to know that there are many friends who grieve with them.

> A protocol of sorts had been established between K Company [his unit] and the German infantrymen on the opposite bank of the [Ruhr River in Germany].

> Several times during our weeks in Lindern, German aidmen had picked up casualties between the lines, and we made it clear to our replacements that nobody was to interfere with such rescue efforts. Special rules of conduct did apply for the wounded.[77]

"The Dogface's Real Hero"

Some of the most overshadowed heroes of war came from the medical corps, the men who provided basic treatment for the wounded during battle. Although they shared every danger with the soldiers, they headed into combat armed only with medical supplies, for medics were not permitted to carry weapons.

Usually each battalion started with thirty to forty medics, but heavy casualties among the group soon lowered that to about one medic for each platoon. Most were youths in their early twenties who either preferred to help their wounded comrades or objected to fighting on religious grounds. Though they refrained from combat, not one soldier ever called them cowardly, for they knew that these unarmed young men faced death and injury to assist the wounded.

Every soldier received combat pay for serving in danger zones, but in an astounding injustice, the government did not hand the medics combat pay because they were technically considered noncombatants. To remedy this situation, men in some units pooled their salaries and handed it to their medics.

Few objected. Of his service in France, Private Byron Whitmarsh said,

> There are worse things than being a rifleman in the infantry, not many, but being a medic is one of them. When the shelling and the shooting gets heavy it is never long until there is a call for "MEDIC!" That's when your regular GIs can press themselves to the bottom of their hole and don't need to go out on a mission of mercy.[78]

The medic's job was to reach a wounded man as quickly as possible following his injury, conduct a hurried examination, apply a tourniquet and inject morphine to dull the pain, clean the wound and sprinkle sulfa powder on it, and drag or carry the soldier to the rear. In frigid weather, some medics carried morphine and plasma under their arms or in their underwear to keep them from freezing.

Sadly, the hazards of being a medic proved all too real. One medic in France listened to a wounded soldier's cries until he could bear it no more. Combat surgeon Brendan Phibbs watched as the medic, named Pico, acted.

> He grabbed a Red Cross flag and ran across the snow waving it. There was no mistaking what he was doing. He was kneeling by the wounded man; he had just given him a shot and was putting on a dressing when the ma-

A medic tends to the wounds of a comrade. The men of the medical corps were the true heroes of the American soldier.

chine gun cut him in two. The German was clearly having a lot of fun because he kept on firing long bursts into the wounded man and into Pico, keeping the bodies jumping and spreading red all over the snow. He'd used the wounded man for bait, an old SS trick.[79]

Another medic named Doc Mellon impressed many soldiers during the fighting in Germany. When a bullet tore through Private Mike Debello's right arm, Mellon hurried to his aid. "Doc Mellon was the bravest kid I ever saw," remembered Debello. "He came running right through the machine-gun fire and put a tourniquet on my arm."[80]

Bill Mauldin recognized these men when he wrote,

> The dogface's real hero is the litter bearer and aid man who goes into all combat situations right along with the infantryman, shares his hardships and dangers, and isn't able to fight back. When the infantryman is down, the medic must get up and help him. That's

not pleasant sometimes when there's shooting.[81]

Treating the Wounded and Dead

Fast, efficient medical assistance for the wounded in World War II saved many lives that would have been lost in earlier wars. An entire network of medical care stretched from the battlefield to hospitals in the United States, and if an injured soldier survived the early moments of his wound, he stood a high chance of living a full life.

The first treatment was administered by the wounded man himself. Each soldier carried medical dressings as part of his gear, and either he or a buddy would apply them. In moments, the unit medic arrived to administer a painkilling medicine and clean the wound. Speed was essential because most men bled profusely, so the quicker the wounded soldier reached an aid station, the better his chances. Surgeons knew that if they could operate within what they called a "golden period"—the six hours after being wounded—the soldier's chances increased dramatically.

Four litter bearers from the forward aid station, which was set up a few hundred yards to the rear, then rushed to the stricken man and hurried him to the aid station.

The wounded man was then rushed to the battalion aid station about one mile back, where doctors administered plasma, removed the bandages and cleaned the wound, made a diagnosis for further treatment, and performed emergency surgery. Staffed usually by two doctors and thirty-six enlisted men, battalion aid stations enjoyed such success that three of every four soldiers returned to duty and 96.5 percent survived. In the Civil War, eighty years earlier, half of the men entering treatment had died.

Physicians were greatly assisted in their efforts by modern drugs and medical techniques. Penicillin became known as the wonder drug for its healing capacities, and plasma kept the soldier alive until he could be operated on. Since the men had gone through rigorous training to become soldiers, their excellent physical condition also helped them survive.

War exacts its toll, of course, so not every man survived before reaching the forward aid station. A soldier was classified as "killed in action" (KIA) if he died of his wounds before reaching the station and as "died of wounds" (DOW) if he died after reaching the aid station.

Forward and battalion aid stations set up wherever they could. Since they were close to the front lines, they frequently had to operate in primitive conditions—an abandoned building that still could be subjected to shelling, a church, or a vacant home. Doc Grizzard treated patients of Company K on the floor of a damaged German farmhouse. As the wounded filtered in, Grizzard and his assistants treated them in the order of severity, American and German wounded alike.

Wounds of All Types

A seemingly endless string of different wounds paraded by physicians in the aid

At a forward aid station, litter bearers fight to save the lives of two men they have evacuated from the battlefield. Speedy treatment was essential to survival.

stations. Dr. William McConahey, a battalion surgeon, recalled of the battle in Normandy, "I've never seen such horrible wounds, before or since. Legs off, arms off, faces shot away, eviscerations [insides hanging out], chests ripped open and so on. We worked at top speed, hour after hour, until we were too tired to stand up—and then we still kept going."[82]

They treated more than gunshot wounds. In fact, more men were put out of action during the incredibly cold winter of 1944–1945 because of trench foot than because of German weapons. More than forty-five thousand soldiers required time away from the front. Trench foot affected feet that were constantly exposed to wet, cold conditions. The soldier first lost his

A Typical Day

Nurses endured a rigorous schedule that kept them on the job nearly around the clock. In his book *Citizen Soldiers,* Stephen Ambrose quotes nurse Ruth Hess, who describes what a typical day was like in her field hospital in France.

> We arrived late in the evening and spent all nite getting ready to receive patients. We worked until 3:00 p.m. Then started nite duty, 12 hours at 7:30 p.m. For nine days we never stopped. 880 patients operated; small debridement of gun shot and shrapnel wounds, numerous amputations, fractures galore, perforated guts, livers, spleens, kidneys, lungs, etc. everything imaginable. We cared for almost 1500 patients in those nine days.

toenails, then his feet turned white, then purple, and finally black. Many lost toes, feet, or even legs to the malady.

Doctors treated many cases of battle fatigue as well. Though some officers tried to claim that battle fatigue was simply a coward's way out of fighting, most soldiers believed not only that it could happen to anyone but that it would occur if a man remained at the front for too long. Infantrymen faced the harsh reality that it was only a matter of time before they were killed, were wounded, or broke down.

With battle fatigue, the soldier first became inattentive to details and walked and spoke in robotic fashion. Tremors or amnesia might set in, and many broke down in uncontrollable sobbing or laughing. Usually, after a bit of rest, hot food, and a change of clothing, the man's spirits recharged and he returned to the front. Of all men evacuated to back area hospitals, one in four was because of battle fatigue.

The only time that soldiers almost enjoyed their stay in a hospital was if they received the "million-dollar wound"—a wound serious enough to get them shipped back home but not so grave that they would be permanently impaired. With this type of injury, the soldier could retain his honor—he left battle because of wounds, not cowardice—and not feel guilty about returning home while his buddies continued to fight. A wound to the buttocks or one that mangled a hand would earn the soldier a trip back to the United States.

One of the worst wounds to receive, from the soldiers' viewpoint, was one that kept them out of action for a month or longer but was not considered serious enough to send them home. When they recovered, these men went into the replacement pool and were shipped to a different unit. If a soldier had to return to combat, he wanted to be with his buddies, so many men begged to get out of the hospital as the fourth week dawned. Some simply got up and left.

George Gieszl, who was wounded near the German border, was approaching the one-month mark when he chatted with a chaplain who tried to convince him that he needed further treatment. Gieszl would have none of it, not only because he did not want to be separated from his unit but because he felt an obligation. "I talked with a chaplain, tried to tell him how I wanted to get back. It was this loyalty thing, *esprit de corps.* I thought they needed me. He didn't understand. He was trying to give me a dose of that bull—. I was telling him, 'I got more important things to do. I got to get back.'"[83]

To the Rear

Ambulances or trains transported the more serious cases to hospitals in Paris or England. One of the first sights that greeted these wounded men was an American nurse, who looked like an angel with her clean uniform and smiling face. The first group of nurses landed at Omaha Beach only four days after American forces assaulted the area on D day. Eventually seventeen-thousand nurses of the Army Nurse Corps served in Europe, and seventeen were killed in combat.

The other sight these men encountered was of a Red Cross volunteer. James Sterner woke up in a hospital to find a member of the Red Cross standing by his bed. She asked the man if he needed a

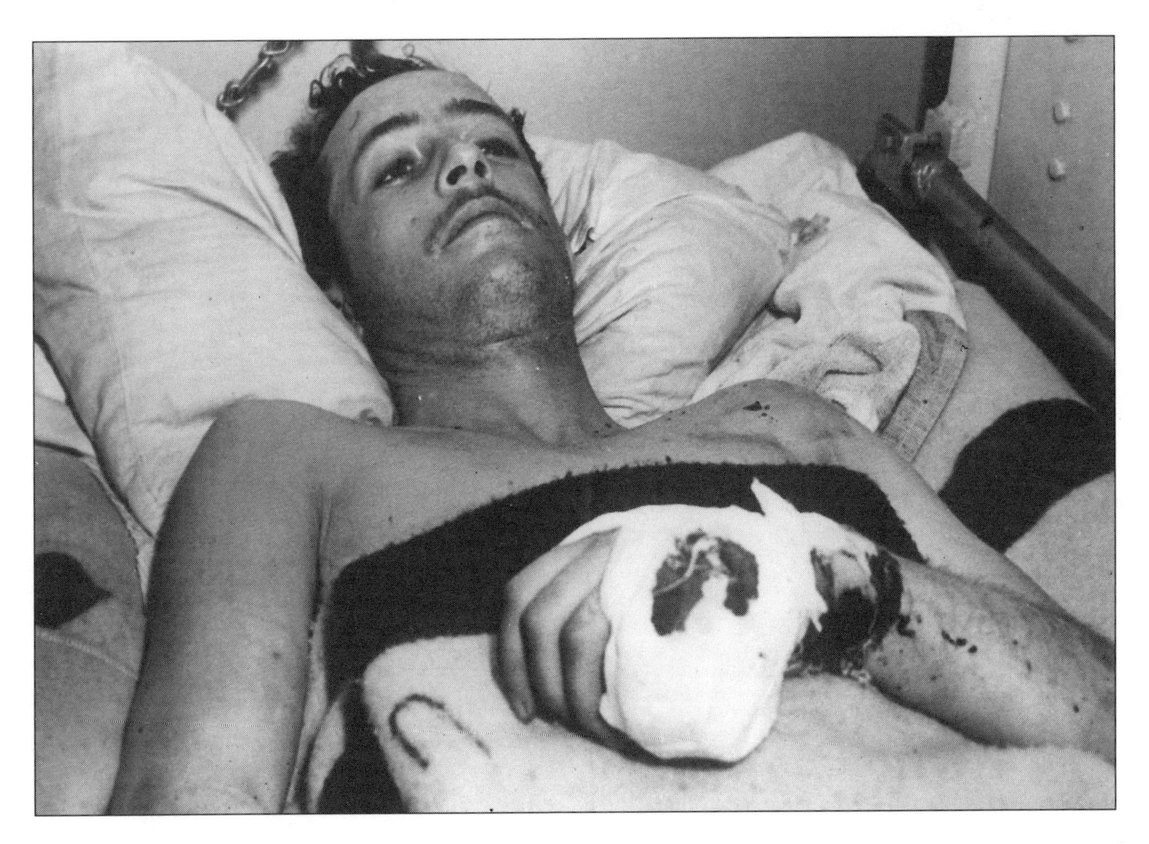

A soldier with a "million-dollar" wound to his hand rests in a hospital before being shipped home.

A Nurse's Prayer

Nurses contributed in so many ways by tending to the wounded under hazardous conditions. They saw and heard things they would carry with them forever. Elizabeth Itzen was so moved by the young infantry soldiers she treated that she wrote the following poem, which appeared in *Yank* magazine and was subsequently reprinted in a 1945 volume, *The Best From* Yank, *the Army Weekly.*

"Good bye," he said, "And thank you nurse,
This has been swell;
But now that I am well again
They'll send me back to hell."

He handed me a [souvenir]
That he had highly prized.
"I know you had your eye on this,
It's a gift from all us guys."

"We're going back to mud knee deep
And cooties in our hair,
And any souvenir like that
Would never help us there.

"I hope you'll say a prayer or two
Not only for me,
But ask the Lord to look out for
The whole darn Infantry."

He turned and swiftly strode away
To join the other guys,
But not before I saw the tears
That welled up in his eyes.

I held the [souvenir] in one limp hand
And watched him out of sight,
And thought of what a kid he was
And how that kid would fight.

So now each night I kneel to pray
And say "God just for me,
Please look out for my patient
And the whole darn Infantry."

Nurses eased the pain and suffering of those injured in battle and were often moved by their patients' gratitude.

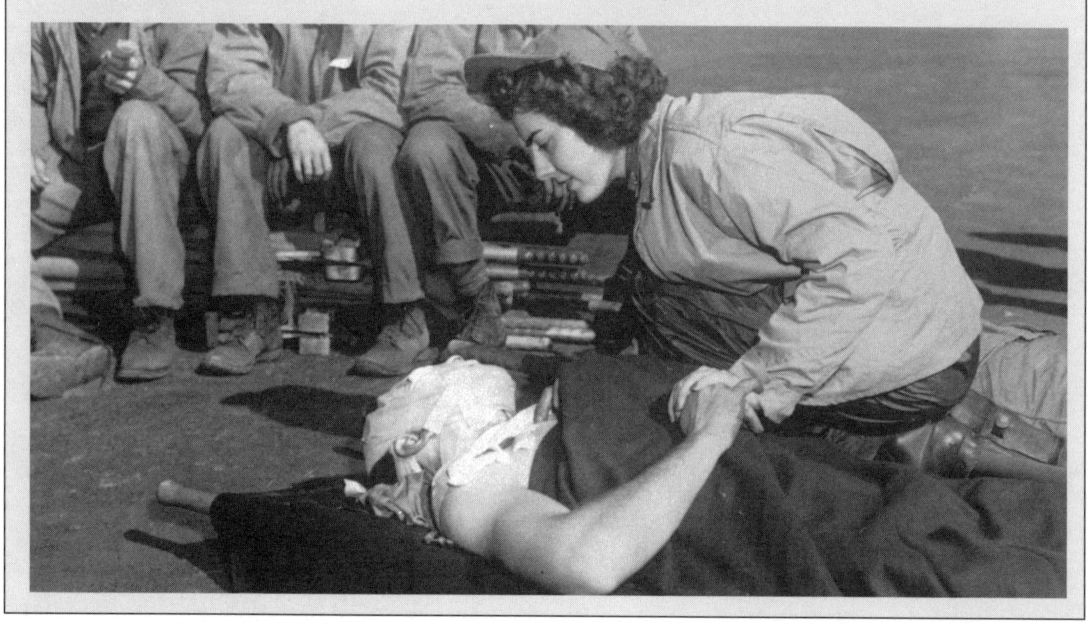

toothbrush, a comb, or anything else. "I've given to the Red Cross every year since," said Sterner. "She was right there."[84]

From the hospitals in Paris or England, the soldier was either released for limited duties, returned to the front, or—if he required more than four months of recuperation—sent home. Speed of medical care often determined who fell into each category. In many cases, less than twenty-four hours elapsed from the time a man was wounded on the battlefield to the time he entered an English hospital.

Company K provides an example of a normal month's activity. In one month's fighting in December 1944 more than 120 men received serious enough wounds or injuries to be evacuated beyond the aid station. Of those, 80 traveled to hospitals in the rear. Half of the 120 suffered from wounds, mostly inflicted by shell fragments; one-fourth suffered frostbite caused by the freezing weather; others headed to the hospital for chest pains, epilepsy, and arthritis; and one soldier entered treatment for a strain caused by lifting five gallons of coffee.

Graves Registration

The support group that few infantrymen envied was the Graves Registration detail, which buried and took care of the remains of the dead. As soon after the battle as possible, Graves Registration personnel scoured the area for bodies and buried them in temporary cemeteries close to the front. If enough was left to identify the remains, one dog tag stayed with the body, and the second was attached to a simple wooden marker or to the man's rifle. That was not always possible, however. "Sure, there were lots of bodies we never identified," stated Sergeant Donald Haguall. "You know what a direct hit by a shell does to a guy. Or a mine, or a solid hit with a grenade, even. Sometimes all we have is a leg or a hunk of an arm."[85]

When the action advanced out of the area, personnel dug up the bodies and reburied them in permanent army cemeteries farther to the rear. Eventually, a stone marker—a cross for Christians, a Star of Israel for Jewish soldiers—rested above the soldier containing his name, rank, serial number, date of birth, and date of death.

Few members of Graves Registration ever adapted to their jobs. Haguall was haunted by one facet.

> The ones that stink the worst are the guys who got internal wounds and are dead about three weeks with the blood staying inside and rotting, and when you move the body the blood comes out of the nose and mouth.
>
> But they all stink. There's only one stink and that's it. You never get used to it, either. As long as you live, you never get used to it. And after a while, the stink gets in your clothes and you can taste it in your mouth.
>
> You know what I think? I think maybe if every civilian in the world could

smell that stink, then maybe we wouldn't have any more wars.[86]

After the war, families of the deceased could have the remains flown home and buried once again in a cemetery of their choice. Many decided to let the remains stay in Europe and rest in the beautifully maintained cemeteries tended by the American Battle Monuments Commission.

The Returnees: The Dead and Wounded

Long before war's end, a lengthy stream of soldiers had been returning to the United States. These were the dead and wounded. For the families of the deceased, it was the beginning of life without their loved one.

The story of Sergeant John A. Bowe Jr.'s family provides an example. It started

American Cemeteries

An often overlooked aspect of war is how the army disposed of the huge numbers of bodies. The army attempted to give each deceased soldier a proper burial. Popular wartime correspondent Ernie Pyle described one cemetery in a column reprinted in David Nichols's book *Ernie's War.*

> The cemetery is neat and its rows of wooden crosses are very white—and it is very big. All the American dead of the beachhead are buried in one cemetery.
>
> Trucks bring the bodies in daily. Italian civilians and American soldiers dig the graves. They try to keep ahead by fifty graves or so. Only once or twice have they been swamped. Each man is buried in a white mattress cover.
>
> The graves are five feet deep and close together. A little separate section is for the Germans, and there are more than three hundred in it. . . .
>
> Even the dead are not safe on the beachhead, nor the living who care for the dead. Many times German shells have landed in the cemetery. Men have been wounded as they dug graves. Once a body was uprooted and had to be reburied.

The American cemetery in Normandy, France.

with the official notification. A soldier arrived at the family home in Worcester, Massachusetts, bearing a telegram from the War Department stating, "THE SECRETARY OF WAR DESIRES ME TO EXPRESS HIS DEEP REGRET THAT YOUR SON SGT JOHN A BOWE JR WAS KILLED IN ACTION IN GERMANY FEB 28 1945."[87]

The family next received a letter from the commander of the soldier's division explaining that Sergeant Bowe was killed while leading his men in an attack against an enemy strong point in the vicinity of Hardt, Germany. The letter added that Bowe's body had been recovered and buried in an American military cemetery in Holland.

A letter from the regimental chaplain expressed regrets and included a package containing the soldier's personal effects, including letters sent to the soldier that arrived after his death. Shortly afterward, the government mailed a series of forms for the next of kin to fill out—one to receive the soldier's final paycheck and another to receive the $10,000 insurance settlement. The government informed the family, "All future communications with reference to this case must bear the File Number XC-3,882,549 and 28N-10,659,747."[88] The soldier who had sacrificed his life was now a number among millions of others.

The wounded arrived throughout the war as well. Families had to adjust to whatever injury the man sustained. Men either became positive contributors to society or wallowed in self-pity and anger.

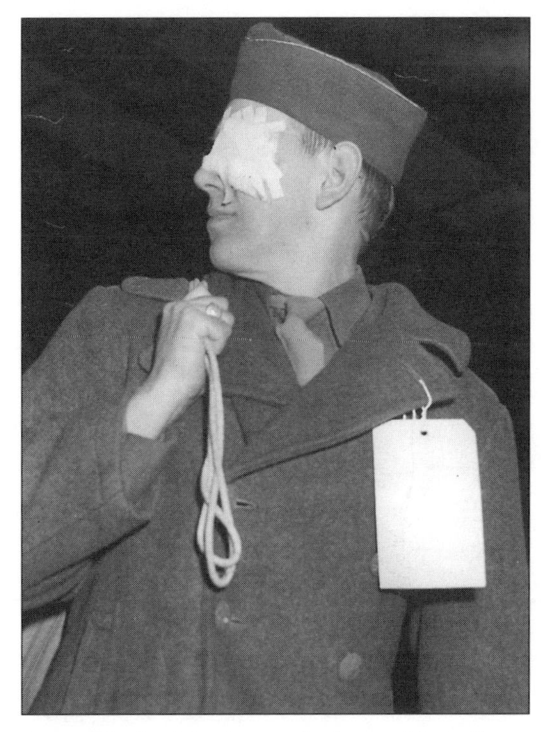

A wounded soldier leaves for home, his smile suggesting that he has adopted a positive approach to dealing with his injury.

Second Lieutenant Paul Leimkuehler and his family exemplified the positive approach so many men adopted. Leimkuehler returned to the United States with his left leg amputated at the knee. When his wife, Kay, traveled to a Virginia hospital for her first visit, she paused to watch another man.

> Paul's mother and I stopped in Washington to change trains. There was a soldier there, an amputee, walking on crutches. I followed him around just to

get myself braced up, because I didn't know what an amputee looked like. I had seen people, but had never really paid much attention to artificial legs or anything like that. So I followed this soldier around just to prepare myself for when I would see Paul.[89]

Her approach helped Paul in overcoming his injury, although the veteran proved that he possessed sufficient strength of his own. Shortly after Paul received an artificial leg, he and Kay invited a group of friends over for Thanksgiving dinner. At first the friends did not know what to say or how to react around Paul, but he dealt with the discomfort in a direct way. According to Kay, "He said, 'You know, you guys have probably never seen an artificial leg.' So he unzipped his pants, took them off, and walked up and down in his shorts, showed them how the leg operated and how the ankle worked, how everything worked. After that, the whole group just sat back in their chairs and heaved a sigh of relief."[90]

When it came to work, Leimkuehler maintained his positive attitude by opening a business selling artificial limbs. Instead of self-pity, he turned what could have been a disadvantage into a way of supporting his family.

The families built on a foundation of love and respect had few problems adjusting to severe injuries. The altered situation brought out the best and, in most cases, strengthened an already stable situation. On the other hand, the wounds tested those families who had problems before the injuries occurred. Some dissolved in divorce and bitterness, others in anger and violence.

★ Chapter 7 ★

"Don't Forget Him—Ever"

When the war in Europe finally ended on May 8, 1945, frontline soldiers erupted in wild celebrations. The one thought that each man had forced out of his mind during the fighting—would he make it out alive—now came rushing to his consciousness in a torrent of emotions. The men had survived, and they could not contain their inexpressible relief and joy.

Men hugged, cheered, and acted like schoolkids on the first day of summer vacation. They disobeyed orders to stand guard duty, which most officers overlooked. One lieutenant stated that for a time the men were "absolutely impossible to control. Their war is over and they don't give a s—for officers, commands, or any of the other trappings of the military."[91]

An officer in the infantry, George Wilson, watched French civilians mingle with his unit on the festive occasion. "The population exploded into the streets and danced and drank the night away amid fireworks and everything else they could cut loose with. Some of us got a little homesick. All of us celebrated on this happy occasion."[92]

Get Me Home!

The soldiers' initial demand was to get them back home. They had agreed to join the military because the Germans had to be stopped, and now that their job was done, they wanted to return home as quickly as possible and resume civilian life. It was almost as if a cloak had been removed from each man to reveal the civilian underneath. He wanted out—now.

The army faced three options. They had to leave some soldiers in Germany as occupation forces, they had to send others to the Pacific to help finish that nasty war, and they could send the rest home. No one wanted to tell a combat soldier who had battled throughout Europe that he now had to travel halfway around the world to enter combat against the Japanese, yet it had to be done.

A Celebration

As American forces swept through France and Italy on their way to Germany, they freed numerous towns and villages. In each municipality, a celebration marked the moment. In his book, *G.I.: The American Soldier in World War II*, Lee Kennett includes the following quote from a citizen of one town who recalled that joyous occasion.

For four years Lagny had been awaiting this moment. A strange sound arose throughout the town. We were free again! In the streets and in all the houses there were cries of joy and excited shouts. People broke out bottles they'd carefully hoarded for the day of victory, and they offered drinks all around. . . . We poured into the streets, into the squares. We laughed, we sang. . . . Hugged and kissed and tugged at, the Americans took it all as best they could. . . . We offered them tomatoes and wine, and they passed to us chewing gum and all sorts of little packages of chocolate and candy and Camel cigarettes—how good they were! They were tired, those poor devils, covered in the dust and sweat and week-old beards, but happiness shone in their eyes.

French citizens greet an American soldier who helped liberate their town from the Germans.

To determine who would be sent home, the army devised a point system. A man received one point for each month in service, one for each month overseas, five points for each campaign, and five points for each combat decoration, such as a Purple Heart for wounds or a Silver Star for valor. Because they wanted to send home as many fathers as possible, the army also awarded twelve points for each child the man had, up to a maximum of three children.

At first the army set eighty-five as the point total needed to be shipped home. If a man fell short of that, he would remain in the army and serve in either Germany or, the one assignment all infantrymen dreaded, the Pacific. However, the American public placed enormous pressure on the military and politicians to get the boys home. Senators in Washington, D.C., received hundreds of pairs of baby shoes with messages pleading that fathers be sent home.

Confident that they could further reduce numbers, the army lowered the point total to eighty in September 1945. When this failed to satisfy the public, the total dropped to sixty in October, then to fifty by December. The army so quickly returned men to civilian life that by the end of 1945 the army's strength had been reduced in half.

Though the system might have seemed fair, many men complained that it favored those units that handed out medals more frequently. The paratroopers, for instance, prided themselves on doing their job without thought of a medal, and thus they were awarded fewer decorations than other companies or battalions. In fact, an office clerk with the 101st Airborne Division usually received the same number of medals as a paratrooper from the same division who fought on a daily basis.

One soldier remembered a paratrooper named MacClung. "MacClung could smell [Germans]; he hunted them; he pursued them in dawn attacks and on night patrols; he went out of his way to kill them; he took more chances and volunteered for more

On board a railway car they have marked with their destinations, soldiers who have earned enough points to go home await departure for a port in France.

dangerous jobs than any other man in E Company. MacClung had made every day of Normandy, Holland, and Bastogne [Battle of the Bulge], and what did he have to show for it?"[93] He and the company clerk accumulated the same point totals, so they both faced being shipped to the Pacific.

To the Pacific

One can hardly imagine the torment the soldiers felt over the prospect of heading to the Pacific to fight the Japanese. However, the army desperately needed more men in the Pacific. Though the war's momentum appeared to favor the United States, few military strategists believed that the Japanese could be defeated without an invasion of Japan itself. Since this enormous undertaking required more men than those who currently served in the Pacific, they had little choice but to transfer troops from Europe.

Those selected to go overseas experienced an emotional roller coaster. After suppressing their feelings during European combat, the men had unleashed their joy in enthusiastic celebration after the war ended. When informed of their Pacific duty, they immediately had to stifle the joyous thoughts and brace themselves for what many considered worse combat conditions than those faced against the Germans. One chaplain watched a transport depart from France in July 1945 on its way to the Pacific and said, "If ever I saw mass misery it was there on Pier F."[94]

Fortunately for the men who battled in Europe, they never had to fire another shot in combat. Before any troop transport arrived in the Pacific, the atom bomb ended the war against Japan. World War II was finally over in both theaters, and men aboard the transports could now completely relax with the thought that they had survived.

Soldiers in Germany

The men who had to remain in occupied Germany struggled with conflicting emotions toward the German people. They commiserated with the lack of basic necessities endured by the Germans. In some places, German civilians placed rows of pots on the ground near American mess tents and quietly waited while the soldiers ate. After they finished eat-

Unlucky Lottery

General Maxwell Taylor, the commanding officer of the paratroopers, spotted the unfairness in the army's point system and ordered that a name be drawn from each company. That man would be sent home. Sergeant Shifty Powers's name was drawn in one company, and though another man offered him $1,000 for the right to go home, Powers turned it down. He and ten other lucky winners, ecstatic that they avoided the fighting in the Pacific, boarded a truck to leave, but along the way the vehicle was involved in an accident. The force of the collision killed one man and tossed Powers out of the truck with such impact that he suffered a number of broken bones. Powers eventually recuperated in a European hospital, but by the time he was strong enough to head home, the other members of his outfit had already returned to the United States because the war had ended in the Pacific.

Fortunately for those selected to go, the atom bomb ended the war with Japan before soldiers could be transferred from Europe to the Pacific.

ing, the Americans emerged and scraped their leftovers into the pots. Some men felt so bad that they returned to the chow line two or three additional times to get more food for the civilians.

On the other hand, the soldiers saw the horrors of the concentration camps. As Captain Belton Cooper of the 3rd Armored Division neared Nordhausen, Germany, with his men, he suddenly noticed that

> a strange apparition emerged from the side of one of the buildings. A tall, frail-looking creature with striped pants and naked from the waist up. It appeared to be a human skeleton with little signs of flesh. The skin appeared to be like a translucent plastic stretched over the rib cage and sucked with a powerful vacuum until it impinged to the backbone in the rear. I could not tell whether it was male or female.[95]

Major Richard Winters approached another concentration camp.

> The memory of starved, dazed men who dropped their eyes and heads when we looked at them through the chain-link fence, in the same manner that a beaten, mistreated dog would cringe, leaves feelings that cannot be described and will never be forgotten. The impact of seeing those people behind that fence left me saying, only to myself, "Now I know why I am here."[96]

American authorities forced German civilians who lived in towns near concentration camps to slowly walk by rows of the emaciated bodies of the dead. General Joseph Collins ordered that every citizen of Nordhausen, Germany, had to bury the bodies found in a nearby concentration camp. General Dwight D. Eisenhower was so stunned by what he saw in a camp at Ohrdruf Nord in Germany that he recommended to President Roosevelt that newspapers send reporters and photographers to record the horror for future generations.

These images angered American soldiers, who as a result treated Germans fairly but sternly during the occupation of the nation. Fearing a possible German resistance movement, American military leaders initially implemented a nonfraternization order—no soldier could have social contact with the German people. When this policy proved hard to enforce, superiors relaxed the requirement.

The Returnees from the Front

Soldiers heading home first traveled to huge processing centers in Europe where they were given a complete physical examination, forms to fill out, and questions to answer. This usually took two or three days. Once the procedures were completed, the soldier boarded a troop transport for the journey across the Atlantic Ocean. After arriving in the United States, where tugboats frequently welcomed the men with water-fountain salutes from fire hoses, the men separated and traveled individually to army camps near their homes for discharge.

Most soldiers pondered the same question asked by families on the home front: Would the returning veteran experience great difficulty with the transition into civilian life? Much had changed in the years since he left for war. Jobs required newer, more advanced skills. Families had grown older. Sons and daughters had matured. Had the veteran missed so much that he was hopelessly behind?

A German girl reels in horror as she is forced to walk past rows of dead concentration camp victims.

On board a troop transport in the Atlantic, soldiers bound for home display a captured German flag. Most veterans wanted to put their wartime experiences behind them.

Aleck Hovsepian, who had seen buddies mangled beyond description and had killed four German soldiers with his bare hands, said, "I've got a lot of things to live down in my soul, a lot of memories to get rid of." When he received his orders home, he wrote, "Today I'm on top of the world. I am going home. I am twice as big as I was, and have glamor and medals all over me. After the hell I've gone through I am a nice guy, I hope, and I know I am a man. But deep inside my soul, I'm scared."[97]

A sergeant explained that "many of us fear that the way of things as we left them will be gone when we again set foot on American soil. We are concerned over the prospect of returning to find our folks, our sweethearts and our friends changed."[98] The one constant for each soldier was home—the thought of it provided sanity in an insane situation. They did not want to find that it had changed when they returned.

Bill Mauldin offered words of assurance to the American public. He claimed that "the vast majority of combat men are going to be no problem at all. They are so damned sick and tired of having their noses rubbed in a stinking war that their only ambition will be to forget it."[99]

Instead, Mauldin explained, what the soldier needed was understanding, sympathy, and a speedy return to normalcy.

> They don't need pity, because you don't pity brave men—men who are brave because they fight while they are scared to death. They simply need bosses who will give them a little time to adjust their minds and their hands, and women who are faithful to them, and friends and families who stay by them until they are the same guys who left years ago.[100]

As soon as the men returned, they usually discarded or stored away all reminders that they had been in the military. Uniforms and medals rested in closets or trunks, and souvenirs found new homes. Those who cared to discuss the war with civilians found an awkward reaction. People hesitated to ask about the war out of fear that it might be too unsettling for the soldier, and veterans hesitated to share their experiences because they knew civilians could never understand.

The first time someone asked Ed Stewart about the war he started to answer, but the person changed the topic when he came to his first graphic description. "So the second time I was asked how it was, I cut myself off after a couple of words."[101]

Most men readjusted to American society with minimal problems. The nation had welcomed the victorious soldiers with open arms, and the strong economy meant that jobs were plentiful. Besides, the government helped by offering the GI Bill of Rights, a law that provided financial assistance for a college education.

Thus most soldiers would later claim that they became better men because of their war experiences and because of the treatment they received afterward. If one speaks to veterans, before long one is bound to hear the sentence, "I'm sure glad I went through the experience, but I wouldn't take a million dollars to repeat it."

However, some returning soldiers struggled with nightmares and anger. Today, those symptoms would be recognized as post-traumatic stress disorder, but in 1945 they were simply signs of readjustment. Aleck Hovsepian said he was "one of those men who look OK on the outside, but are empty and aching inside, a sort of walking ghost full of memories that shouldn't have happened to them."[102]

Changes

African-American soldiers returned to an improved economic situation, but they also reentered a society that considered them second-class citizens. This was especially hard to endure for the soldiers who spent much time in France, where bigotry toward blacks was almost nonexistent. Frustrated at once again being in the throes of segregation, many African-American soldiers joined the civil rights movement to fight for better treatment. They had risked their lives for democracy, and now they demanded equal treatment at home.

Other combat soldiers had seen too much to be content with their previous lives. An infantryman from a rural area stated, "I never got much more than 15 miles from home. The Army's taken me through 15 countries from Brazil to Iceland and from Trinidad to Czechoslovakia. After where I've been and what I've seen, I couldn't settle down on any farm."[103]

George Lucht had starred as the football captain and quarterback of a college team before the war and intended to resume the sport once he returned. An unexpected occurrence happened, though. "I began to play first-team football again. About halfway through the season, however, I lost all interest in aggressive behavior. I thought, the hell with it. It wasn't that important to me."[104]

Memories

Since 1945 the soldiers who fought in Europe have dealt with the memories of war in various ways. Some openly discussed their experiences; most remained relatively quiet. Through the years, more turned to each other for companionship and comfort, mainly by attending annual reunions of survivors' associations.

Orval Faubus explained why these steps proved so valuable.

> We weren't homesick for the hardships of training or the dangers of battle, we concluded, but there were some things

"Only Centimeters Decided"

Studs Terkel is a renowned interviewer and writer from Chicago, Illinois, who has published a string of successful books about epochs in U.S. history. In his book, *The Good War,* Terkel talked with veterans about their experiences. One soldier related the following.

> I live life as if presented to me. I'm surprised that I have it. A friend asked me, "What's your attitude toward death?" It is absolutely zero. With much more surprise and excitement, I take the fact that I'm alive. I look at my children and my grandchildren and I think: only centimeters decided whether they should be on this earth or not. Whether the bullet went that way or this way. They don't understand that they live on this earth quite by accident. It was quite natural that I wouldn't be alive. But I lived and they happened.

A lucky soldier examines a bullet hole in his helmet.

we missed in civilian life which we had known with our fellow soldiers. We were lonesome for the unequaled fellowship we had found in the ranks of our comrades. We missed the pleasure of the deep and abiding friendships.[105]

In Normandy, France, a veteran stands with his son and grandson during ceremonies marking the fiftieth anniversary of the invasion.

National holidays to honor veterans, especially Memorial Day, became more important to them as a way to honor their efforts and their fallen comrades. They see that the comforts and joys of today's society occurred, in large measure, because of the sacrifices that they and their friends made. They do not wish to be forgotten.

Bill Mauldin had the final word.

When you lose a friend you have an overpowering desire to go back home and yell in everybody's ear, "This guy was killed fighting for you. Don't forget him—ever." Keep him in your mind when you wake up in the morning and when you go to bed at night. Don't think of him as the statistic which changes 38,788 casualties to 38,789. Think of him as a guy who wanted to live every bit as much as you do. Don't let him be just one of "Our Brave Boys" from the old home town, to whom a marble monument is erected in the city park, and a civic-minded lady calls the newspaper ten years later and wants to know why that "unsightly stone" isn't removed.[106]

Notes

Introduction: "The Sharp End"

1. Quoted in Gerald F. Linderman, *The World Within War: America's Combat Experience in World War II.* New York: Free Press, 1997, p. 4.
2. Quoted in Linderman, *The World Within War,* p. 312.
3. John Ellis, *The Sharp End: The Fighting Man in World War II.* New York: Charles Scribner's Sons, 1980, p. 12.

Chapter 1: "I Can Take Anything"

4. Quoted in Lee Kennett, *G.I.: The American Soldier in World War II.* New York: Charles Scribner's Sons, 1987, p. 33.
5. Quoted in Kennett, *G.I.,* p. 37.
6. Quoted in Stephen E. Ambrose, *Band of Brothers.* New York: Simon & Schuster, 1992, pp. 16–17.
7. Quoted in Kennett, *G.I.,* p. 54.
8. Quoted in Kennett, *G.I.,* p. 55.
9. Harold P. Leinbaugh and John D. Campbell, *The Men of Company K: The Autobiography of a World War II Rifle Company.* New York: William Morrow, 1985, p. 11.
10. Leinbaugh and Campbell, *The Men of Company K,* pp. 11–12.
11. Ambrose, *Band of Brothers,* p. 19.
12. Quoted in Ambrose, *Band of Brothers,* p. 26.
13. Ambrose, *Band of Brothers,* p. 15.

Chapter 2: "Our New-Boy Illusions . . . Dissolved"

14. Quoted in Stephen E. Ambrose, *D-Day, June 6, 1944: The Climactic Battle of World War II.* New York: Simon & Schuster, 1994, p. 322.
15. Quoted in Ambrose, *D-Day,* p. 354.
16. Quoted in Ambrose, *D-Day,* p. 329.
17. Quoted in Ambrose, *D-Day,* p. 356.
18. Quoted in Linderman, *The World Within War,* p. 20.
19. Quoted in Linderman, *The World Within War,* p. 15.
20. Quoted in Stephen E. Ambrose, *Citizen Soldiers.* New York: Simon & Schuster, 1997, p. 264.
21. Quoted in Linderman, *The World Within War,* p. 22.
22. Leinbaugh and Campbell, *The Men of Company K,* p. 37.
23. Quoted in Linderman, *The World Within War,* p. 12.
24. Quoted in John C. McManus, *The Deadly Brotherhood: The American Combat Soldier in World War II.* Novato, CA: Presidio Press, 1998, p. 149.
25. Quoted in Linderman, *The World Within War,* p. 13.

26. Quoted in Linderman, *The World Within War*, p. 76.
27. Quoted in Linderman, *The World Within War*, pp. 26–27.
28. Quoted in Linderman, *The World Within War*, pp. 20–21, 29.
29. Quoted in Kennett, *G.I.*, p. 172.
30. Quoted in Linderman, *The World Within War*, p. 55.

Chapter 3: "They Stay and Fight"

31. Quoted in Ambrose, *Citizen Soldiers*, p. 73.
32. Quoted in Kennett, *G.I.*, p. 137.
33. Quoted in Linderman, *The World Within War*, p. 262.
34. Robert Sherrod interview by author, Washington, DC, 15 July, 1991.
35. S. L. A. Marshall, *Men Against Fire.* New York: William Morrow, 1947, p. 43.
36. Quoted in Linderman, *The World Within War*, p. 272.
37. Bill Mauldin, *Up Front.* New York: Henry Holt, 1945, p. 14.
38. Mauldin, *Up Front*, p. 14.
39. Quoted in McManus, *The Deadly Brotherhood*, p. vi.
40. Quoted in Linderman, *The World Within War*, p. 347.
41. Mauldin, *Up Front*, p. 16.
42. Quoted in McManus, *The Deadly Brotherhood*, p. 244.
43. Quoted in McManus, *The Deadly Brotherhood*, p. 243.
44. Mauldin, *Up Front*, pp. 19–20.

Chapter 4: Fighting Other Enemies

45. Quoted in Robert Leckie, *Delivered from Evil.* New York: Harper & Row, 1987, p. 630.
46. Quoted in Martin Blumenson, *The United States Army in World War II: Salerno to Cassino.* Washington, DC: Office of the Chief of Military History, 1969, p. 286.
47. Quoted in McManus, *The Deadly Brotherhood*, p. 50.
48. Quoted in Editors of *Yank*, *The Best from* Yank, *the Army Weekly.* New York: E. P. Dutton, 1945, p. 48.
49. Quoted in Ambrose, *Citizen Soldiers*, p. 169.
50. Quoted in McManus, *The Deadly Brotherhood*, p. 51.
51. Ambrose, *Citizen Soldiers*, p. 345.
52. Bernard C. Nalty, *Strength for the Fight: A History of Black Americans in the Military.* New York: Free Press, 1986, p. 163.
53. Quoted in Studs Terkel, *The Good War: An Oral History of World War II.* New York: Pantheon Books, 1984, p. 151.
54. Quoted in Ambrose, *Citizen Soldiers*, pp. 346–47.
55. Quoted in McManus, *The Deadly Brotherhood*, p. 246.
56. Quoted in Editors of *Yank*, *The Best from* Yank, *the Army Weekly*, p. 214.
57. Quoted in Editors of *Yank*, *The Best from* Yank, *the Army Weekly*, p. 215.

Chapter 5: Support from the Military and from Home

58. Quoted in Ambrose, *Citizen Soldiers*, p. 112.
59. Quoted in McManus, *The Deadly Brother-*

hood, p. 104.
60. Quoted in McManus, *The Deadly Brotherhood*, p. 105.
61. Quoted in Ambrose, *Citizen Soldiers*, p. 252.
62. Quoted in Ambrose, *Citizen Soldiers*, p. 253.
63. Quoted in Ambrose, *Citizen Soldiers*, p. 271.
64. Quoted in Linderman, *The World Within War*, pp. 25–26.
65. Quoted in Kennett, *G.I.*, p. 147.
66. Quoted in Linderman, *The World Within War*, p. 317.
67. Quoted in Ambrose, *Citizen Soldiers*, p. 335.
68. Quoted in Kennett, *G.I.*, p. 89.
69. Quoted in Kennett, *G.I.*, p. 73.
70. Paul Fussell, *Wartime: Understanding and Behavior in the Second World War*. New York: Oxford University Press, 1989, p. 145.
71. Quoted in Linderman, *The World Within War*, p. 319.
72. Quoted in Linderman, *The World Within War*, p. 322.
73. Mauldin, *Up Front*, pp. 129–30.

Chapter 6: "Missions of Mercy"

74. Quoted in Terkel, *The Good War*, p. 380.
75. Quoted in Linderman, *The World Within War*, p. 140.
76. John A. Vietor, *Time Out: American Airmen at Stalag Luft I*. New York: Richard R. Smith, 1951, p. 143.
77. Leinbaugh and Campbell, *The Men of Company K*, p. 216.
78. Quoted in Ambrose, *Citizen Soldiers*, pp. 313–14.
79. Brendan Phibbs, *The Other Side of Time: A Combat Surgeon in World War II*. Boston: Little, Brown, 1987, p. 138.
80. Quoted in Leinbaugh and Campbell, *The Men of Company K*, p. 233.
81. Mauldin, *Up Front*, p. 118.
82. Quoted in Ambrose, *Citizen Soldiers*, p. 327.
83. Quoted in Leinbaugh and Campbell, *The Men of Company K*, p. 198.
84. Quoted in Leinbaugh and Campbell, *The Men of Company K*, p. 200.
85. Quoted in Frank Brookhouser, ed., *This Was Your War*. New York: Dell, 1960, p. 495.
86. Quoted in Brookhouser, *This Was Your War*, p. 495.
87. Quoted in Leinbaugh and Campbell, *The Men of Company K*, p. 245.
88. Quoted in Leinbaugh and Campbell, *The Men of Company K*, p. 246.
89. Quoted in Leinbaugh and Campbell, *The Men of Company K*, p. 250.
90. Quoted in Leinbaugh and Campbell, *The Men of Company K*, p. 252.

Chapter 7: "Don't Forget Him—Ever"

91. Quoted in Linderman, *The World Within War*, p. 232.
92. George Wilson, *If You Survive*. New York: Ivy Books, 1987, p. 257.
93. Quoted in Ambrose, *Band of Brothers*, p. 290.
94. Quoted in Linderman, *The World Within War*, p. 232.

95. Quoted in Ambrose, *Citizen Soldiers*, p. 461.
96. Quoted in Ambrose, *Citizen Soldiers*, p. 464.
97. Quoted in Linderman, *The World Within War*, pp. 357–58.
98. Quoted in Linderman, *The World Within War*, p. 306.
99. Mauldin, *Up Front*, pp. 9–10.
100. Mauldin, *Up Front*, p. 11.
101. Quoted in Linderman, *The World Within War*, p. 327.
102. Quoted in Linderman, *The World Within War*, p. 358.
103. Quoted in Kennett, *G.I.*, p. 231.
104. Quoted in Leinbaugh and Campbell, *The Men of Company K*, pp. 279–80.
105. Quoted in Kennett, *G.I.*, p. 239.
106. Mauldin, *Up Front*, p. 57.

★ Chronology of Events ★

1929

The Geneva Convention produces a list of "rules" governing warfare.

1940

On September 16, President Franklin D. Roosevelt signs into law the Selective Training and Service Act, thereby bringing the draft to the nation.

1941

On December 7, the United States enters World War II when Japan attacks the naval base at Pearl Harbor, Hawaii.

1942

The Women's Auxiliary Army Corps is established; in November, the first large number of American soldiers enters battle with the invasion of North Africa.

1943

In June, the Women's Army Corps opens the army to women; in July, American soldiers begin a lengthy fight to push the German army out of Italy.

1944

In June, President Roosevelt signs the GI Bill of Rights, thereby guaranteeing certain benefits to returning soldiers; on June 6, D day brings American forces to the European mainland; in October, the first African-American units enter combat; in December, the Battle of the Bulge produces heroic fighting between American and German troops; on December 17, eighty American prisoners are gunned down in the Malmédy massacre; the bitterly cold winter of 1944–1945 produces forty-five thousand cases of trench foot.

1945

On May 8, the war in Europe ends; on August 15, the war in the Pacific ends; soldiers begin returning to the United States according to the army's point system, which drops to fifty by December; by year's end, the army is reduced by half.

✯ For Further Reading ✯

John Morton Blum, *V Was for Victory.* New York: Harcourt Brace Jovanovich, 1976. This examination of the American home front is especially helpful in its analysis of how Americans viewed the war.

Frank Brookhouser, ed., *This Was Your War.* New York: Dell, 1960. This collection of some of the finest examples of wartime reporting provides a touching and thorough view of World War II.

Michael D. Doubler, *Closing with the Enemy.* Lawrence: University Press of Kansas, 1994. An excellent account of the fighting in Europe compiled by a lieutenant colonel in the army.

Morris Fishbein, ed., *Doctors at War.* New York: E. P. Dutton, 1945. An excellent survey of every aspect of medical treatment in the war.

James Jones, *WWII.* New York: Grosset and Dunlap, 1975. Written by an acclaimed novelist who fought in the war, this book contains some of the best explanations of soldiers' behavior found in literature. Though Jones focuses on the Pacific Theater, his conclusions are equally valid for Europe.

Charles B. MacDonald, *Company Commander.* Washington, DC: Infantry Journal Press, 1947. This is an excellent volume that depicts what life was like for an officer in the war.

Audie Murphy, *To Hell and Back.* New York: Henry Holt, 1949. This memoir by the war's most decorated soldier delivers a fascinating view of life for a combat soldier.

Geoffrey Perret, *There's a War to Be Won.* New York: Random House, 1991. Writing with an easy style, the author presents a gripping account of the U.S. Army in World War II.

Brendan Phibbs, *The Other Side of Time: A Combat Surgeon in World War II.* Boston: Little, Brown, 1987. Written by a physician, this book delivers some helpful information about the surgeon's role in World War II.

Colin Shindler, *Hollywood Goes to War.* London: Routledge & Kegan Paul, 1979. A decent short summary of how the film industry presented the war to the American public and how it promoted the war in its pictures.

James Tobin, *Ernie Pyle's War.* Lawrence: University Press of Kansas, 1997. A good biography of the war correspondent that includes helpful information on the man and the war.

John A. Vietor, *Time Out: American Airmen at Stalag Luft I.* New York: Richard R. Smith, 1951. Vietor, a prisoner of war, provides a superb glimpse of life in a German prison camp.

George Wilson, *If You Survive.* New York: Ivy Books, 1987. Written by an infantry officer, this book includes useful material on fighting the war.

✯ Works Consulted ✯

Stephen E. Ambrose, *Band of Brothers.* New York: Simon & Schuster, 1992. Written by one of the war's most revered historians, this book follows one airborne company from training, through entry into battle on D day, and to war's end; it looks at war through the eyes of the combat soldier.

————, *D-Day, June 6, 1944: The Climactic Battle of World War II.* New York: Simon & Schuster, 1994. Another fine volume by the leading historian that details the events surrounding D day.

————, *Citizen Soldiers.* New York: Simon & Schuster, 1997. A gripping account of the fighting in Europe, told mainly from the combat soldier's point of view.

Martin Blumenson, *The United States Army in World War II: Salerno to Cassino.* Washington, DC: Office of the Chief of Military History, 1969. This volume in the acclaimed series of histories assembled by the U.S. Army following World War II describes the fighting in Italy.

John Costello, *Virtue Under Fire.* Boston: Little, Brown, 1985. The author presents an interesting account of how the war changed views toward social attitudes.

Editors of *Yank, The Best from* Yank, *the Army Weekly.* New York: E. P. Dutton, 1945. This book is indispensable in describing what war was like for the combat soldier and what thoughts occupied his mind. This collection of articles, poems, and cartoons from the weekly publication *Yank* was written by soldiers about soldiers.

John Ellis, *The Sharp End: The Fighting Man in World War II.* New York: Charles Scribner's Sons, 1980. Although this book concentrates mainly on the experiences of British soldiers, it contains valuable material and conclusions that apply equally as well to the American fighting man.

Paul Fussell, *Wartime: Understanding and Behavior in the Second World War.* New York: Oxford University Press, 1989. A university professor who commanded men in World War II and was seriously wounded delivers an enlightening look at the war.

Lee Kennett, *G.I.: The American Soldier in World War II.* New York: Charles Scribner's Sons, 1987. An outstanding depiction of what life was like for soldiers in World War II.

Clayton R. Koppes and Gregory D. Black, *Hollywood Goes to War: How Politics, Profits, and Propaganda Shaped World War II Movies.* New York: Free Press, 1987. The authors examine the motives behind movies made during World War II and help the reader understand the connection between national priorities and what Hollywood produced.

Robert Leckie, *Delivered from Evil.* New York: Harper & Row, 1987. A well-written general history of World War II compiled by a veteran of the war.

Harold P. Leinbaugh and John D. Campbell, *The Men of Company K: The Autobiography of a World War II Rifle Company.* New York: William Morrow, 1985. Two men who battled across Europe present their story in this gripping narrative that offers an "insider" view of life in a rifle company.

Gerald F. Linderman, *The World Within War: America's Combat Experience in World War II.* New York: Free Press, 1997. A superb account of combat in World War II that draws from soldiers' letters and recollections.

S. L. A. Marshall, *Men Against Fire.* New York: William Morrow, 1947. An authoritative account of men in battle by an esteemed military historian; it helps clarify why and how men fight.

Bill Mauldin, *Up Front.* New York: Henry Holt, 1945. If you want a view of war from the foxhole, this book is indispensable. Written and drawn by a famous wartime cartoonist, it follows the daily events in the lives of two fictional soldiers—Willie and Joe. No soldier who fought in World War II has forgotten this extraordinary pair of cartoon figures.

John C. McManus, *The Deadly Brotherhood: The American Combat Soldier in World War II.* Novato, CA: Presidio Press, 1998. A solid depiction of life for soldiers in World War II.

Joe Morella, Edward Z. Epstein, and John Griggs, *The Films of World War II.* Secaucus, NJ: Citadel Press, 1973. A fascinating book about the movies made during World War II and the viewpoints expressed by them, many of which examine the role of the soldier. The book not only provides information but is fun to read.

Bernard C. Nalty, *Strength for the Fight: A History of Black Americans in the Military.* New York: Free Press, 1986. An official government military historian, Bernard Nalty has assembled the complete story of segregation and integration in the armed forces.

David Nichols, ed., *Ernie's War: The Best of Ernie Pyle's World War II Dispatches.* New York: Simon & Schuster, 1986. The only contemporary comparable to Bill Mauldin is newspaper reporter Ernie Pyle, who, in his columns, attempted to give readers some idea of what life was like for the combat soldier.

Ernie Pyle, *Brave Men.* New York: Henry Holt, 1944. Published during the war, this collection of Ernie Pyle's columns vividly brought the war in Europe to readers in the United States. Along with Bill Mauldin's cartoons, Pyle's writing delivers the best description of war for the front-line soldier.

Studs Terkel, *The Good War: An Oral History of World War II.* New York: Pantheon Books, 1984. One of the best interviewers in the nation presents a series of discussions he conducted with veterans of the war; this easy-to-read volume contains much valuable information.

✯ Index ✯

☆ Picture Credits ☆

Cover photo: Digital Stock
Archive Photos, 10, 14, 20, 23, 31, 53
Associated Press/Dreamworks, 7 (bottom)
Brown Brothers, 72, 77, 79
Corbis, 24, 34, 51, 89
Corbis/Owen Franken, 87, 96
Corbis/Hulton-Deutsch Collection, 11, 17, 33, 35, 39, 47
Corbis/Museum of Flight, 59
Corbis/Michael St. Maur Sheil, 84
Corbis-Bettmann, 7 (top), 8, 12, 38, 43, 45, 49 (both), 54, 62, 74, 82, 88, 95
Digital Stock, 5, 21 (both), 25, 36, 41, 91
FPG International, 13 (both), 15, 16, 57, 60, 65, 66, 67, 81, 85, 93
Lambert/Archive Photos, 58, 70
pixelpartners, 27, 28, 30, 40, 46, 64, 73, 92

✯ About the Author ✯

John F. Wukovits is a junior high school teacher and writer from Trenton, Michigan, who specializes in history and biography. Besides biographies of Anne Frank, Jim Carrey, Stephen King, and Martin Luther King Jr. for Lucent, he has written biographies of the World War II commander Admiral Clifton Sprague, Barry Sanders, Tim Allen, Jack Nicklaus, Vince Lombardi, and Wyatt Earp. A graduate of the University of Notre Dame, Wukovits is the father of three daughters—Amy, Julie, and Karen.